Battle of the Boyne 1690

The Irish campaign for the English crown

Battle of the Boyne 1690

The Irish campaign for the English crown

Michael McNally · Illustrated by Graham Turner

Series editor Lee Johnson

First published in Great Britain in 2005 by Osprey Publishing, Midland House, West Way, Botley, Oxford OX2 0PH, United Kingdom.
443 Park Avenue South, New York, NY 10016, USA
Email: info@ospreypublishing.com

ISBN 1 84176 891 X

Design by The Black Spot
Index by David Worthington
Maps by The Map Studio Ltd.
3D bird's eye views by The Black Spot
Battlescene illustrations by Graham Turner
Originated by PPS-Grasmere, Leeds, UK
Printed in China through World Print Ltd.

05 06 07 08 09   10 9 8 7 6 5 4 3 2 1

A CIP catalogue record for this book is available from the British Library.

For a catalogue of all books published by Osprey please contact:

NORTH AMERICA
Osprey Direct, 2427 Bond Street, University Park, IL 60466, USA
E-mail: info@ospreydirectusa.com

ALL OTHER REGIONS
Osprey Direct UK, P.O. Box 140 Wellingborough, Northants, NN8 2FA, UK
E-mail: info@ospreydirect.co.uk

www.ospreypublishing.com

Dedication

To my wife Petra, and children Stephen and Elena-Rose for putting up with 'the budding author' over the last year.

Acknowledgements

I'd like to thank Andy Copestake, Ian Spence, Jurrien de Jong, Robert Hall, Dr David Murphy and Dr Bill Maguire who all gave of their time and patience to answer queries and make suggestions where needed, as well as Jane Bohan who agreed to drive me around the Boyne Valley in order to take a number of photographs, some of which are reproduced here. Again, thanks to Robert Hall and Soren Henriksen for their help with uniform and equipment details, and for producing the colour uniform plates for the book. Finally, a word of thanks to Lee Johnson and Marcus Cowper for commissioning the title and making sense of my ramblings respectively.

Artist's note

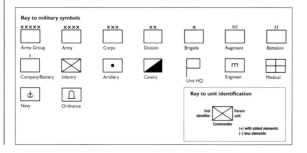

CONTENTS

ORIGINS OF THE CAMPAIGN

THE ACCESSION OF KING JAMES II

After a reign of almost a quarter of a century, King Charles II of England died on 6 February 1685. In the main, his rule had been a successful one, healing the wounds of the Civil War and Protectorate; and yet, in the final analysis he failed his people by being unable to provide the country with a legitimate heir. Instead, his successor would be his younger brother, James, Duke of York.

James, aged 51, was in many ways the complete opposite of his elder brother – where Charles would dissemble, James could not or would not; and whilst the elder trusted few people, the younger trusted all, and in this trait lay the seeds of the events of 1688.

Apart from a minor insurrection in Scotland, the first challenge to the new regime came in June 1685 when an illegitimate son of Charles II, James Scott, the Duke of Monmouth, landed in south-west England, accusing James not only of fratricide but also of arson on the grandest scale imaginable – the Great Fire of London! Inevitably supporters began to flock to Monmouth's banner, and at Taunton in Somerset he proclaimed himself King James II, declaring his uncle's coronation to be invalid as a result of his Catholicism.

This second rebellion soon went the same way as the first, and at the disastrous battle of Sedgemoor on 6 July 1685, the rebels were scattered and Monmouth captured. The Duke pleaded for clemency and was brought before the King. His pleas fell on deaf ears and he was beheaded on Tower Hill on 15 July.

Before Monmouth was cold, a series of courts – the 'Bloody Assizes' – were established to try those rebels who had so far escaped summary execution and any who had allegedly aided and abetted them. Absolute government had again reared its head in England and this, rather than religion, became the focus of opposition to James.

THE 'GLORIOUS REVOLUTION' OF 1688

Since the early 1670s, Western Europe had been polarized into two distinct political groupings as a result of the policies of King Louis XIV. Rulers would either support France for their own political or financial gain or, alarmed by French expansion, would attempt to form a unified front against France. An example of the former was King Charles II of England, who by secret treaty received a regular subsidy from the French treasury in order to secure English participation in an anti-Dutch alliance. Examples of the latter were obviously those states such as Spain, the Hapsburg Empire and the German Rhineland

OPPOSITE, TOP **The birth of the Prince of Wales, 10 June 1688. The birth of a male heir was the catalyst for William of Orange's invasion. With a Catholic succession in England secured, any hopes that William had of gaining the throne through his wife, the Princess Mary, were dashed. The only remaining alternative was war. (Collection Ulster Museum Belfast, courtesy Trustees NMGNI)**

OPPOSITE, BOTTOM **The landing of William III at Torbay. Originally planning to land on 4 November, his birthday and wedding anniversary, William missed his landfall and landed the following day. His supporters made capital of this delay, as his landing coincided with the anniversary of the Gunpowder Plot – a Catholic-inspired attempt to kill King James I and blow up the Houses of Parliament. (With kind permission of the Trustees, Atlas Van Stolk, Rotterdam)**

principalities whose lands bordered France, and were thus potential targets of French aggression.

There was another nation which, although not sharing a common border with France, had become the opponent of the French crown – the United Dutch Provinces, a Protestant mercantile state whose overseas empire rivalled that of France. This in itself was not total anathema to the court at Versailles, as many of the Dutch elite were inclined to closer ties with France. However, a new political party was coming to the fore, led by William, Prince of Orange, whose family had for many years been Stadtholders (chief magistrates) of several of the Dutch provinces.

William's chance came in 1672 when the French invaded the United Dutch Provinces. Following the overthrow of the Dutch government, he was appointed Captain-General and Admiral for life. In a desperate war for survival, William thwarted the French by opening the dykes and flooding the country around Amsterdam.

In 1677, and possibly to counter any claims of Catholic subversion in Whitehall, King Charles II arranged the marriage of his niece Mary, the eldest daughter of the Duke of York and therefore Charles's second heir, to her cousin William, and this became the basis of his future claim to the English crown. James was not happy with the match, but obeyed his brother's wishes and allowed the marriage to go ahead.

Peace with France was signed in 1678 but did not last long, for in 1680 French troops marched into the principality of Orange and, under the guise of removing a potential rallying point for French Huguenots, annexed it to the French crown. William saw this as a direct attack on himself, and from this time onwards he dedicated himself to thwarting Louis's ambitions using his not inconsiderable diplomatic skills to forge an anti-French coalition, known as the League of Augsburg, which comprised a number of those states who had reason to fear French aggression.

Despite the impressive number of allies, which already comprised Austria-Hungary, Brandenburg, Spain, Sweden and, informally, the United Dutch Provinces, William of Orange was painfully aware that the biggest asset was missing: without England and her navy, no such union would have a realistic chance of success.

Upon the death of King Charles II in 1685, William felt that the reign of his Catholic father-in-law, James II, would be simply a momentary diversion and that his wife would soon be crowned Queen Mary II. However, James soon weathered the storm of the Monmouth and Argyll rebellions and although public opinion went heavily against him in the aftermath of Monmouth's execution and the 'Bloody Assizes', he was still relatively secure on his throne. William decided that something needed to be done to undermine James's position.

Encouraged by his negotiations with English dissidents, he therefore developed a plan based around two central factors – an invasion of England to secure the throne in his wife's name, and the defence of the United Dutch Provinces. For the first to succeed, the second must be assured.

The birth of the Prince of Wales in June 1688 virtually destroyed William's plans by removing his wife from the direct line of succession, but, armed with the assurances of his English contacts who had contrived to cast doubt on the young prince's legitimacy, he felt that this could be overcome.

By the middle of October, all was ready. On the 19th, William boarded his flagship *Den Briel*, but adverse weather conditions held the ships in port until 1 November. Then, borne by a 'Protestant wind', the fleet made headway into the Maas estuary and thence out to sea.

Across the Channel frantic preparations were taking place. With several Irish and Scots regiments transferred to England, James would be able to call upon something in the region of 50,000 men, comfortably outnumbering William's forces, but with the need to cover several potential landing sites, this numerical superiority was greatly diluted. James's preparations were mainly intended to cover the northern and eastern coasts of England, with the fleet under the Earl of Dartmouth taking station off the Essex coast, from where he could engage William's ships.

During the voyage William received intelligence of James's dispositions and accordingly the fleet changed direction, heading for the Straits of Dover. Then the true nature of the 'Protestant wind' revealed itself, for whilst it blew William's armada towards its intended destination, it also held the English fleet in a vice-like grip, forcing Dartmouth to watch impotently as the enemy sailed off into the English Channel.

William made landfall at Torbay on 5 November, and immediately set out towards London and a confrontation with his father-in-law. Once the landing became public knowledge, the first desertions started to appear in James's army but the King, in an apparent show of strength, began to redeploy his forces. After garrisoning London, the main force of 24,000 men marched to Salisbury. A series of skirmishes ensued, but then came news of mutinies and defections throughout the north of the country. James's nerve failed, and on 22 November he ordered his army to withdraw towards Reading.

Several individuals who had up until now sat on the fence jumped into William's camp, fewer than expected but crucially including senior officers such as John Churchill (the future Duke of Marlborough) and the Duke of Grafton, James's nephew. Appalled by the treachery of many of those whom he trusted, James's determination collapsed like a house of cards and he fled, arranging for his wife and son to be taken to France for their safety.

In theory at least, William was now master of the country but, even in defeat James's bad luck held and he was captured on the Kent coast on 11 December and taken to Faversham. William was in a quandary: his opponent had lost but he himself had not yet won, for whilst James remained in the kingdom, he was still *de jure* King of England. The only resolution was for James to be allowed to escape the country, effectively abdicating the throne. On 18 December 1688, as William triumphantly entered London, James was en route for France accompanied by his son the Duke of Berwick. He would never see England again.

TYRCONNEL'S RISE

Since the middle of the 17th century, the situation in Ireland had been volatile indeed. When Oliver Cromwell had been unable to discharge his army following the defeat of the Irish Catholic Confederacy, he made up the arrears in their pay by awarding them land that had been confiscated from the Catholic rebels in lieu of cash. This, the 'Cromwellian Land

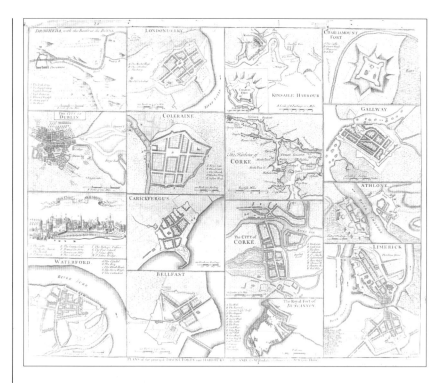

Plan of the Principal Towns, Forts and Harbours in Ireland. Unlike Continental Europe, there had been no 'military revolution' in Ireland, and thus many fortifications were decades out of date and had to be hastily improved with temporary works. (Courtesy of the National Gallery of Ireland, Dublin)

Settlement', was to be further complicated upon the Restoration of King Charles II in 1660. Many Catholic landowners had supported the Stuarts throughout their exile and, having suffered for their loyalty, not unreasonably looked forward to a restoration of their lands and possessions that had been taken from them during the Commonwealth and Protectorate. Their aspirations were soon dealt a cruel blow as Charles's military support came, in the main, from those selfsame soldiers who had fought for Cromwell. Whilst he appreciated the loyalty of the Irish Lords, Charles was unable and unwilling to alienate his new-found supporters and, inevitably, the compromise which was embodied in the Restoration Land Settlement pleased few of the petitioners and only served to exacerbate the situation. The Duke of Ormonde was quoted as saying that the only way to resolve the problem was to find two Irelands, each of which would need to be bigger than the original!

Needless to say, the bulk of Irish Catholics began to look forward to the accession of James, Duke of York, who as a Catholic could be relied upon to enact polices that would be beneficial to his co-religionists, and, indeed, shortly after James's coronation it was obvious that moves were being made to change the political situation in Ireland. Firstly the Duke of Ormonde, the incumbent Lord Lieutenant was recalled and replaced by two Lord Justices appointed to lead the administration until such time as a replacement was announced. But of more importance was the news that two prominent Catholic officers, Justin MacCarthy and Richard Talbot, were being appointed to the command of units that had previously been the province of Ormonde and his son, the Earl of Arran.

The rebellions of 1685 had illustrated the unreliability of the regional militias, and therefore, given his reluctance to have armed troops over which he had no direct control, James decided to disarm them and to store their weapons in royal arsenals.

In Ireland, this duty fell to Colonel Talbot and he set about his task with quiet efficiency, safe in the knowledge that no Catholics would be disadvantaged by his actions, as the Irish militia was a wholly Protestant formation. In June 1685, in recognition of past and present services, he was elevated to the Irish Peerage as Earl of Tyrconnel.

Ormonde's successor was James's brother-in-law Henry Hyde, Earl of Clarendon, and whilst it outwardly seemed that the situation in Ireland was unchanged, the King's plans to develop an army loyal to himself rather than to parliament soon began to take shape. In early 1686 Tyrconnel was promoted Lieutenant General and Marshal of Ireland – effectively the commander of the Irish army – and the links between the civil and military administrations were severed.

By the time Clarendon took office, Tyrconnel had already been hard at work 'remodelling' the Irish army, establishing his own clientele of mainly Catholic, Anglo-Irish officers, many of whom were tied to him by friendship or marriage.

Assured of his position and unable and unwilling to work with the Viceroy, Tyrconnel spent the latter part of 1686 lobbying for Clarendon's recall, and within a year he had secured victory over his rival, being granted the lesser title of 'Lord Deputy'.

THE RETURN OF KING JAMES

The collapse of King James's government had left Tyrconnel in a difficult situation: William's success had led to unrest amongst Irish Protestants at a time when fully half of the army – mainly the better-trained regiments – had been transferred to England and subsequently incarcerated by the new regime. Fortunately for James, many were able to make their escape and in time return to Ireland, either directly or via France, but the writing on the wall was plain, Ireland was militarily bankrupt, and unless measures were taken, all that Tyrconnel had achieved would be undone.

James II landing at Kinsale by Adriaan Schoenebeek. James was the first English monarch to set foot on Irish soil for over three centuries. To the Irish, he was their legitimate sovereign who would redress all wrongs. To William's supporters he had already abdicated and the Irish Jacobites were simply rebels. (Collection Ulster Museum Belfast, courtesy Trustees NMGNI)

Indeed, William's advisors continually pressed him to move against Ireland as quickly as was practical, but with the position in England still unsure, dialogue was opened with Dublin to investigate the likelihood of a political settlement. What was needed was a suitable envoy, and in a demonstration of synchronicity, such a man was already a prisoner in William's hands: Colonel Richard Hamilton was one of James's most trusted and proven officers, but his main asset lay not in his undoubted military ability, but rather in his family connections in Ireland.

Sending Hamilton was a disaster for William; on his arrival at Dublin Castle he appraised Tyrconnel of the confused and chaotic situation in England, and urged him to press James to take up arms to regain his throne, but the question was how best to prepare for the inevitable conflict?

Firstly, and under the pretence that he was still willing to negotiate with William, Tyrconnel sent a deputation headed by Lord Mountjoy, a potential leader of the Irish Protestants, to France, allegedly to ask for instructions but in truth to arrange for Mountjoy's imprisonment in the Bastille and to procure military supplies from King Louis XIV.

Secondly, and in order to counter the lack of manpower, he did the only thing possible in the circumstances, and appealed to the Gaelic-Irish, also Catholics, for their support. In his letter to James, dated 29 January 1689, he wrote:

> There are four Regiments of Old Troopes, and one Battalion of the Regiment of Guards and three Regiments of Horse with one Troop of Grenadiers on Horseback. I have given out Commissions for neare forty Regiments of Foot, four Regiments of Dragoons and two of Horse, all of which amount to neare 40,000 men, who are all uncloathed and the greatest part unarmed, and are to be subsisted by their severall officers untill the last of February next out of their owne purses, to the ruine of most of them; but after that day I see no possibility for arming them, clothing them or subsisting them for the future but abandoning the Country to them: but after all if I may be supplied by the last of March with these succours that are necessary which I press in my letters, I doubt not that I shall preserve this Kingdome entirely for Your Majesty.

The nucleus of an army was there, but without adequate supplies and above all money to pay the troops, it would dissolve, and any hope that Tyrconnel had of achieving his long-term aims would be lost. At this point, the French King intervened and two officers were sent to Ireland to review the situation and report back to Versailles. Already a plan was developing in Louis's mind: although not a gifted soldier, William was an exceptionally charismatic leader and thus the longer that he could be diverted from the Continent, the better it would be for France. The report decided that with the necessary support, the Irish would be able to defend themselves against invasion from Britain, and on the strength of this assertion the French government sent an initial consignment of 8,000 matchlocks, albeit of dubious quality, to help arm the Irish.

This was not good enough for Tyrconnel as, with King James in France, there was no way he could legitimately alter the status quo in Ireland; to do anything he needed the presence of the King on Irish soil and, eventually succumbing to pressure from both Dublin and Versailles, James agreed to lead the expedition. Vauban, the celebrated

French engineer, summed up James's position quite succinctly when he wrote: 'I have an idea that when a man plays his last stake he ought to play it himself or to be on the spot. The King of England seems to be in this condition. His last stake is Ireland.'

On 12 March 1689, James landed at Kinsale and, upon his arrival, the Jacobite command began to polarize. His English and Scots followers generally favoured a resolution in Ireland that would enable them to transfer the main theatre of operations to Scotland and thence to England, whilst his Irish supporters obviously favoured a more definite solution to their own situation before any other options should be considered. Of a more neutral aspect were the coterie of French advisors who had travelled in his suite: the Comte d'Avaux, Louis's envoy to the Jacobite court; and Generals de Rosen, de Maumont and de Pusignan; the former to act as King Louis's eyes and ears in Ireland, and the latter three to lead and train the Jacobite forces.

THE CAMPAIGN

THE CONFLICT BEGINS

Even as Tyrconnel consolidated his position in Dublin, pockets of resistance began to spring up across the country – whether prompted by religious conviction, fear of losing property and estates or simply out of loyalty to King William – but by the time of James's landing, the last such area outside of Ulster, Bandon, in County Cork, had been reduced by troops commanded by Justin MacCarthy.

Resistance in the north, was widespread, centred mainly around Derry, Enniskillen, Hillsborough and Sligo, and in the first weeks of 1689 these 'armed associations' drove off many isolated detachments of Tyrconnel's army. A 'Council of the North' was established at Hillsborough, headed by the Earl of Mountalexander, who was appointed to command all Protestant forces in Counties Antrim, Armagh, Down and Monaghan. Dialogue was opened up with the other main centres of resistance, and envoys despatched to London to request armed support.

Shortly after the coronation of William and Mary in London, the Council decided to attack the Jacobite garrison of Carrickfergus. The attack was a failure, and its sole result was to illustrate to the Dublin government just how unprepared the Ulstermen were for war.

Fully aware that action needed to be taken to restore the situation in Ulster, Tyrconnel issued a statement on 7 March offering a pardon to those under arms who returned to the King's Peace. To reinforce the proclamation, Richard Hamilton, newly promoted to lieutenant general, was sent northwards with a mixed force of around 2,500 men to pacify the countryside.

Tyrconnel's demands were refused and a force of troops under Sir Arthur Rawdon was sent to bar Hamilton's progress. On 14 March 1689, the two forces faced each other at the village of Dromore in County Down, but before combat could be joined, the Protestants turned and fled the field.

Although the 'Break of Dromore', as it became known, effectively gave eastern Ulster to the Jacobites it was not the end, for Rawdon was able to gather a large number of armed men and reinforce the garrison of Coleraine as Hamilton's forces looted their way through the province.

Waves of refugees were swept before the advancing Jacobites. The more affluent were able to flee the country, seeking asylum in England or Scotland, whilst the majority simply made for the fortified towns of Coleraine, Derry and Enniskillen. Macaulay, in his *History of England*, conjures up a vivid picture:

The flight became wild and tumultuous, the fugitives broke down the bridges and burned the ferryboats. Whole towns, the seats of Protestant

MILITARY SITUATION IN IRELAND: JANUARY–JUNE 1689

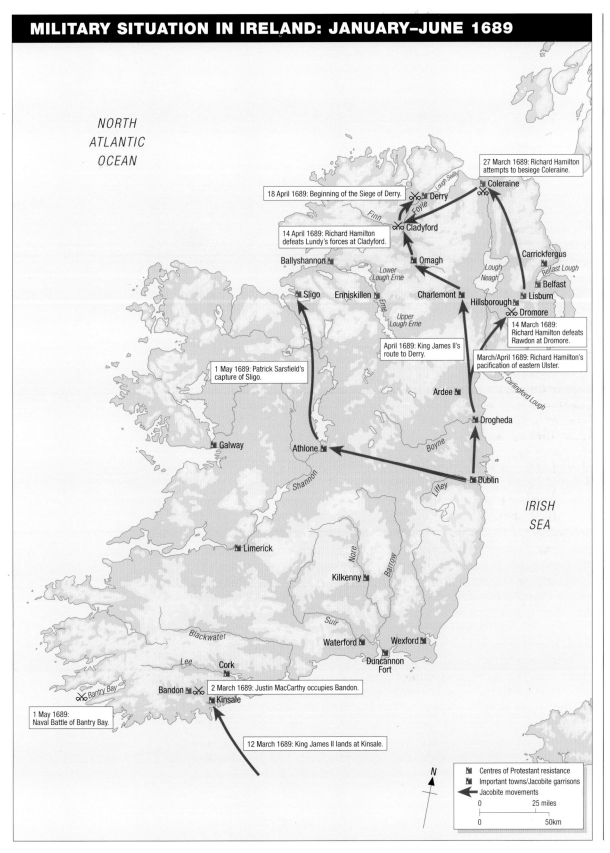

NORTH
ATLANTIC
OCEAN

27 March 1689: Richard Hamilton attempts to besiege Coleraine.

18 April 1689: Beginning of the Siege of Derry.

14 April 1689: Richard Hamilton defeats Lundy's forces at Cladyford.

Coleraine

Derry

Lough Swilly

Foyle

Finn

Cladyford

Carrickfergus

Belfast Lough

Ballyshannon

Omagh

Lower
Lough Erne

Lough
Neagh

Belfast

Lisburn

Sligo

Enniskillen

Charlemont

Hillsborough

Dromore

Erne

Upper
Lough Erne

14 March 1689:
Richard Hamilton defeats
Rawdon at Dromore.

April 1689: King James II's
route to Derry.

March/April 1689: Richard Hamilton's
pacification of eastern Ulster.

1 May 1689: Patrick Sarsfield's
capture of Sligo.

Carlingford Lough

Ardee

Drogheda

Galway

Athlone

Boyne

Shannon

Dublin

IRISH
SEA

Liffey

Limerick

Nore

Barrow

Kilkenny

Suir

Blackwater

Waterford

Wexford

Lee

Cork

Duncannon
Fort

Bantry Bay

Bandon

2 March 1689: Justin MacCarthy occupies Bandon.

Kinsale

1 May 1689:
Naval Battle of Bantry Bay.

12 March 1689: King James II lands at Kinsale.

N

Centres of Protestant resistance
Important towns/Jacobite garrisons
Jacobite movements

0   25 miles

0   50km

population, were left in ruins without one inhabitant. The people of Omagh destroyed their own dwellings so utterly that no roof was left to shelter the enemy from the rain and wind. The people of Cavan migrated in one body to Enniskillen. The day was wet and stormy. The road was deep in mire. It was a piteous sight to see, mingled with the armed men, the women and children, weeping, famished and toiling through the mud up to their knees.

Hamilton's army deployed before Coleraine on 27 March and, unable to prosecute a formal siege, he immediately sent a summons for surrender, hoping that the events of the previous weeks would have unnerved the garrison who, for their part, were determined to give a better showing than at Dromore.

The summons was refused and at 10.00am on the following morning, the Jacobite artillery opened up a bombardment of the town, and Hamilton's infantry began to inch forward. For the rest of the day the firefight continued, with the defenders claiming to have killed over 60 Jacobites for the loss of only three of their own.

Unwilling to become bogged down, Hamilton decided to press on towards Derry, reasoning that if Coleraine's garrison stayed put, their position would become untenable and that they would eventually need either to surrender or abandon the town. Continually probing westwards, the Jacobite forces crossed the Bann at Portglenone on 7 April.

As anticipated, Coleraine was indefensible, and the troops there fell back to Derry before their line of retreat was finally cut. Both sides paused and took stock of the situation: the Protestants continued their appeals to London, and began to prepare themselves for the inevitable siege, whilst in the Jacobite camp fissures began to appear.

THE WALLS OF DERRY

In November 1688 and in order to strengthen his control over the north, Tyrconnel withdrew Mountjoy's regiment from garrison duty in Derry and attempted to replace it with that of the Earl of Antrim. Needless to say, the civic authorities, whilst unwilling to have Catholic troops billeted upon them, were wary of thwarting the crown. However, events soon overtook both lord deputy and city council, for even as Antrim's 'Redshanks' were approaching the Ferry Gate, a group of young apprentices seized the keys to the city gates, slamming them in the soldiers' faces and locking them out of the city.

In an attempt to retrieve the situation, Mountjoy was ordered back to Derry, and when the gates remained shut, he reached a compromise whereby two companies of Protestant troops under Lieutenant Colonel Robert Lundy would be permitted to enter the city and act as garrison. A veteran soldier, Lundy immediately began preparations for the city to withstand a siege: recruiting troops, modernizing defences, laying in supplies. Although he would later be regarded as a traitor, it was Lundy's foresight in these early days that ensured the survival of the city.

In April 1689, as Richard Hamilton's forces closed in on the city from the east, a third Jacobite army started its march on Derry, comprising much of the Dublin garrison and led by King James in person, determined to restore his authority in the north.

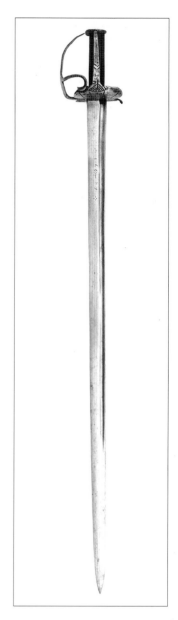

Sword, English, late 17th century. This plainly decorated cavalry sword has a 3ft-long blade of which only part of the upper side is ground to an edge in order to assist in penetration when thrust at an enemy. (Photograph courtesy of the Trustees, Royal Armouries, Leeds)

Conscious of the ever-tightening noose, an attempt was made on 14 April to stall the Jacobite advance. Lundy led the bulk of his forces from the city to prevent the enemy from securing the crossings over the river Finn. Contemptuous of the Irish troops, and believing that he could halt the Jacobites with firepower, he fatally misjudged the Irish horse, and at Cladyford his forces were broken by the Jacobite cavalrymen. It was at this time that a message was received from Derry with news that an English fleet had arrived with reinforcements and supplies.

A council of war was rapidly convened, and, his personal morale shattered by the reverse at Cladyford, Lundy persuaded the relieving forces that Derry was indefensible and that they should withdraw; he then opened negotiations with Hamilton to discuss the surrender of the city. In the circumstances, the Jacobite terms were exceedingly fair – a general pardon and restitution for all damage incurred. To this, Hamilton added the codicil that his forces would remain in position and not approach the city whilst the terms were being considered. He knew that his troops were not in a position to besiege Derry, and thus he was prepared to offer any reasonable inducement to ensure a capitulation.

Many inside the walls were inclined to accept Hamilton's offer. However, on 18 April, fate took a hand when James arrived at the Bishop's Gate on the southern side of the city, at the head of a force arriving from Dublin. Amid cries of 'treachery', the gates were slammed shut and, almost immediately, the walls belched fire, the resulting cannonade killing or seriously wounding several of James's staff. Even as James rode away from the walls, the weather broke, and this would play an important factor in the coming months.

The events of the 18th spelt the end for Lundy, and a council of war persuaded him to quit the city – there would be no surrender.

Initially, the command of James's forces at Derry fell to the French general, de Maumont, seconded by his countryman, de Pusignan, as well as Richard Hamilton and the Duke of Berwick. From Berwick's own memoirs, it would appear that the initial plan was to maintain a strict

KING JAMES BEFORE THE GATES OF DERRY, 18 APRIL 1689 (Pages 18–19)

Following his victory at Cladyford on 15 April 1689, Lt. Gen. Richard Hamilton opened negotiations for the surrender of Derry, with the strict provision that his forces would not advance any closer to the city whilst negotiations were underway. Unaware of the ceasefire that had been put emplaced, King James arrived before the city on 18 April, at the head of a column of Jacobite reinforcements, and rather than skirt the city at a distance he rode up to the walls with a small escort, and called upon the defenders to surrender. The King is shown here (1) in a red statecoat, and with the blue sash of the Order of the Garter.

Seeing a large body of enemy troops advancing upon them and fearing treachery, the city gates were slammed shut, and the troops manning the defences opened fire on James's party – the defenders were unaware of the identity of their target, and a formal apology was later sent to King James by Derry's governing council. In the ensuing chaos, one of James's aides, Captain Troy was hit by round shot and killed (2). Immediately James's escorts tried to get the King to retire to safety and in the foreground, unsure of the situation, we see an officer of James's Foot Guards (3) attempting to steady his men. To the right of the picture, we see further Jacobite infantry awaiting orders, including Lord John Bellew's regiment of foot (4). From the beginning of hostilities, the Derry garrison under Robert Lundy had been working to improve their outdated defences – strengthening the walls, and building an outwork or ravelin (5) to protect the Bishop's Gate. Dominating the city wall we see the tower of St Columb's Cathedral (6), which was used both as an observation platform and an artillery position. Above the tower flies a crimson flag, a symbol that there would be no surrender. As King James withdrew from the Bishop's Gate, and now with no hope of a negotiated settlement, the Jacobite forces began to formally invest the city, in a siege that would last over a hundred days. (Graham Turner)

blockade of the city until such time as sufficient men and *matériel* had been gathered to allow the prosecution of a formal siege.

Disaster struck almost immediately when, on 21 April, Adam Murray, one of the more enterprising Loyalist officers, led a raid on the Jacobite position at the Pennyburn Mill. As soon as he heard of the attack, de Maumont raced to the scene at the head of a troop of horse whilst further reinforcements were being gathered, but was killed within moments of engaging the enemy. As additional troops arrived, Murray withdrew, hotly pursued by the Jacobites, who were then ambushed by a force of infantry that had been deployed to cover his eventual retreat.

Two days later, Murray launched another raid on the enemy lines, and, as the Jacobites began to concentrate their numbers, further fierce fighting took place around Pennyburn – several officers including de Pusignan and the Duke of Berwick were casualties, the former succumbing to his wounds allegedly as a direct result of the ministrations of an Irish surgeon. King James's army had disastrously lost two commanding officers in almost as many days.

Command now devolved upon Richard Hamilton, one of whose first acts was to make a formal report to Dublin requesting reinforcements of both men and *matériel*. However, events were not only favouring the defenders, as Berwick was able to capture an outpost at Culmore, by a *ruse de guerre*. The loss of the fort was of crucial importance to both sides, as it commanded the narrows of the Foyle to the north of the city, and from this position Hamilton directed the construction of a boom and several artillery positions to seal the river and prevent waterborne reinforcement from reaching Derry's river quays.

As the boom was being completed, Hamilton launched another assault upon Windmill Hill. This attack, better planned than the first, made use not only of combined arms, but also of converged grenadier companies whose task was to act as assault troops and seize the enemy outworks. Initially the Jacobites swept all before them and it seemed as if fortune had

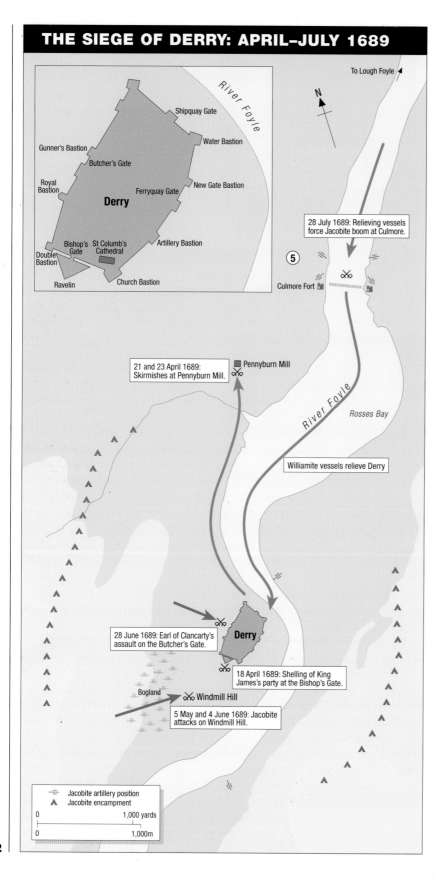

THE SIEGE OF DERRY: APRIL–JULY 1689

River Foyle

Shipquay Gate

Water Bastion

Gunner's Bastion

Butcher's Gate

Royal Bastion

New Gate Bastion

Ferryquay Gate

Derry

Bishop's Gate

St Columb's Cathedral

Double Bastion

Artillery Bastion

Ravelin

Church Bastion

To Lough Foyle

N

28 July 1689: Relieving vessels force Jacobite boom at Culmore.

(5)

Culmore Fort

xxxxxxxxxxxxx

21 and 23 April 1689: Skirmishes at Pennyburn Mill.

Pennyburn Mill

River Foyle

Rosses Bay

Williamite vessels relieve Derry

28 June 1689: Earl of Clancarty's assault on the Butcher's Gate.

Derry

18 April 1689: Shelling of King James's party at the Bishop's Gate.

Bogland

Windmill Hill

5 May and 4 June 1689: Jacobite attacks on Windmill Hill.

Jacobite artillery position

Jacobite encampment

0   1,000 yards

0   1,000m

Derry – St Colomb's Cathedral. The cathedral steeple had not been built at the time of the siege and, commanding the walls, the flat tower was used as both an observation post and an artillery position from which to bombard the besiegers. (Author's photograph)

finally smiled upon them, but she is a fickle mistress. According to Captain Ash, one of the Loyalist officers present: '[grenadiers] came over the bog, near the Double Bastion and beat our men thence, all but a little boy, who when they were climbing the trenches stood stoutly upon the trench and threw stones at them. Our men being then reinforced from the city came down with spirit and beat them quite over the meadows.'

Four days later came the first indications that the defenders of Derry were no longer alone – an English warship, *Greyhound*, entered the Foyle and attempted to force the boom. The vessel ran aground during an exchange of fire, but with luck was able to refloat herself and escape further damage. In his official report, the ship's captain greatly exaggerated the strength of the Jacobite position and as a result of this, a relief force under Percy Kirke, after arriving in Lough Foyle, subsequently diverted to Inch Island, further down the coast in Lough Swilly, to await further clarification of the defenders' situation.

After this, things returned to a stalemate, with neither side being able to gain the initiative, but shortly before the end of June, the experienced French general, de Rosen, returned to the city.

On 28 June, a further assault was launched on the southern part of the city, with the objective of destroying a series of outworks that had been built to protect the Butcher's Gate, and if possible to storm the gate which had already taken some damage. The troops chosen for the operation were from the Earl of Clancarty's regiment, which was relatively fresh and virtually up to strength. It was the last major engagement of the siege, and probably the fiercest fighting. As in the second assault on Windmill Hill, the Jacobites initially carried all before them, but even as they reached their objective the defenders launched a final, desperate counter-attack and threw them back with heavy losses on both sides.

Frustrated by this reverse, de Rosen issued the orders that have earned him a degree of infamy: local Protestants were herded into the no man's land between the besiegers and the besieged, in the hope that their co-religionists would not allow them to starve, thus placing an ever greater strain on Derry's already precarious supply problems.

Disgusted by de Rosen's actions, Hamilton complained directly to King James, and the Frenchman was relieved of his command, eventually returning to France. After de Rosen's departure, the Jacobites again began negotiations for the surrender of the city, but by now Kirke had re-entered Lough Foyle and, under pressure to act decisively, he dispatched the frigate *Dartmouth* and three merchantmen – *Phoenix*, *Jerusalem* and *Mountjoy* – laden with troops and supplies to force the boom.

On the evening of 28 July, with *Jerusalem* being held back until the boom had been breached, *Dartmouth* cast off and led the other two vessels into the gauntlet of roundshot. Approaching the defences, the frigate came under fire from the shore batteries but shielded the two

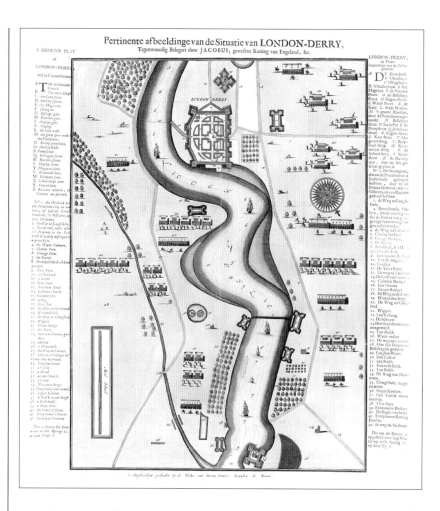

merchantmen, allowing them to take a 'run' at the boom. Assisted by ships' boats full of sailors with axes, the *Mountjoy*, the heavier of the two, sheared through the logs and, despite the gunnery from the shore, broke through the boom. The route to the city was clear.

For three days following the initial relief, an uneasy tension existed, with both sides occupying their positions, but on 31 July, realizing that it was now impossible to take the city, Hamilton withdrew his forces. The city had held out for 105 days, and whilst it was no siege by the criteria of the day, those who manned the walls felt it to be so and as such it must be judged.

THE WAR IN THE WEST

As Richard Hamilton's troops marched northwards into Ulster, further forces were being sent into the west in an attempt to roll up other Protestant enclaves. A column under Pierce Butler, Viscount Galmoy, was dispatched to secure Enniskillen, whilst a larger force commanded by Patrick Sarsfield was ordered to take Sligo.

After an abortive attempt to take Enniskillen, Galmoy retreated into County Cavan, but Sarsfield was able to march into Sligo virtually unopposed. However, on the advice of local sympathizers, he then squandered his success by attempting to take the town of Ballyshannon, at

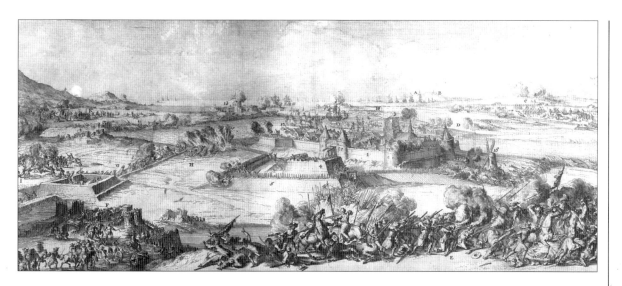

Siege of Londonderry by Romeyn de Hooghe. (Collection Ulster Museum Belfast, courtesy Trustees NMGNI)

the mouth of the Erne, Enniskillen's lifeline to the sea. Not for the first time was Jacobite intelligence found to be lacking – Ballyshannon was heavily fortified and more than a match for the Jacobite artillery. This was only the beginning of Sarsfield's problems, as word soon reached him that over 1,000 men were marching against him from Enniskillen under the command of Thomas Lloyd, a one-time subordinate of his.

As reports of Lloyd's progress increased, Sarsfield crossed the Erne, taking up position on some rising ground surrounded by bog, blocking the enemy's advance and forcing him to attack across adverse terrain. Despairing of the alternatives, Lloyd set his men to making fascines, which were to be thrown out in front of his troops in order to make crossing the marsh easier, and as this work continued he had a stroke of luck – one of his scouts had come across a local man who was able to lead the Williamites through the bog.

Believing the enemy to be withdrawing, the Jacobites began to howl and jeer at them, but it soon became clear to Sarsfield that the enemy was outflanking his position. The cavalry was ordered to intercept Lloyd's men, but too late, and, as the Enniskilleners began to form up on firmer ground, Sarsfield gave the order to retreat. Order soon gave way to chaos, and, although the bulk of his forces reached Sligo and safety, many were captured and sent as prisoners to Enniskillen.

It was a bad start to the campaign and affairs soon degenerated into raid and counter-raid and, as the Jacobite noose around Derry tightened, an abortive attempt was made to relieve the city from Enniskillen. From this point it was realized that both Loyalist enclaves would have to rely on their own resources for their survival.

In order to finally reduce Enniskillen, Tyrconnel decided to concentrate as much of the army as possible in the Erne Valley. The Duke of Berwick was sent southwards from Derry to liaise with Sarsfield's forces, but again the defences were found to be too tough a nut to crack. Conscious of the need to do something, Berwick wrote to Sarsfield in Sligo, ordering him to Ballyshannon, where their forces would unite, and together they would seize the river port.

Accordingly, Sarsfield marched southwards, but as he came within a few miles of Ballyshannon, he received news that the Duke had retired **25**

to Derry. Unsupported, he successfully beat off an enemy attack on his encampment near Lough Melvin, and sending messages to Anthony Hamilton and Justin MacCarthy, Viscount Mountcashel, he proposed a combined attack on Enniskillen in overwhelming force.

The two correspondents did indeed unite their forces but their orders were to attack post-haste and therefore, without reference to Sarsfield, began their advance upon the town, eventually coming up against the Williamite position at Crom Castle. Led by one of James's most experienced commanders, it would have been better in hindsight for the Jacobites to have either bypassed or masked Crom, but at the time and for various reasons it was decided that only a frontal assault would suffice.

Initially all went well, as Jacobite troops stormed the outworks, but then disaster struck as Mountcashel lost control of the situation, and in a frenzy his men pursued their opponents up to the castle walls. Running straight into a curtain of enemy fire, they took heavy casualties before falling back and regrouping for an assault on the following day.

The failure to keep Sarsfield informed of his intentions was about to have serious consequences for Mountcashel, as this vital reinforcement remained inactive, threatening neither Ballyshannon nor the enemy shipping on the Erne. This not only allowed the Williamites to move with relative impunity, but it also led to reinforcement from Lough Swilly and the arrival of a small cadre of experienced officers, one of whom, Colonel William Wolseley, would soon prove himself to be one of the better commanders on either side during the war.

Wolseley decided to attack Mountcashel's forces before he could unite with Sarsfield, and at Lisnaskea the advance guards of both forces met. Initially the Jacobites seemingly had the upper hand but were lured into an ambush and badly mauled by the Enniskillen cavalry. With his mounted troops scattered in all directions, Mountcashel withdrew northwards to the village of Newtownbutler, where the terrain was more conducive to defence.

The Jacobites deployed south of the town where the Enniskillen road traversed a hill surrounded by an area of bog. Reasoning that this terrain

The Relief of Derry by William Sadler. A stylized version of events, this picture shows English warships under full sail breaking through the boom. In reality the deed was accomplished by ships' boats full of sailors armed with axes, hammers and other tools. (Collection Ulster Museum Belfast, courtesy Trustees NMGNI)

Derry – the south-eastern wall. With insufficient artillery or siege equipment to breach the walls of Derry, the Jacobites would be forced to rely on bombardment or escalade to take the city. (Author's photograph)

MILITARY SITUATION IN IRELAND: JULY–DECEMBER 1689

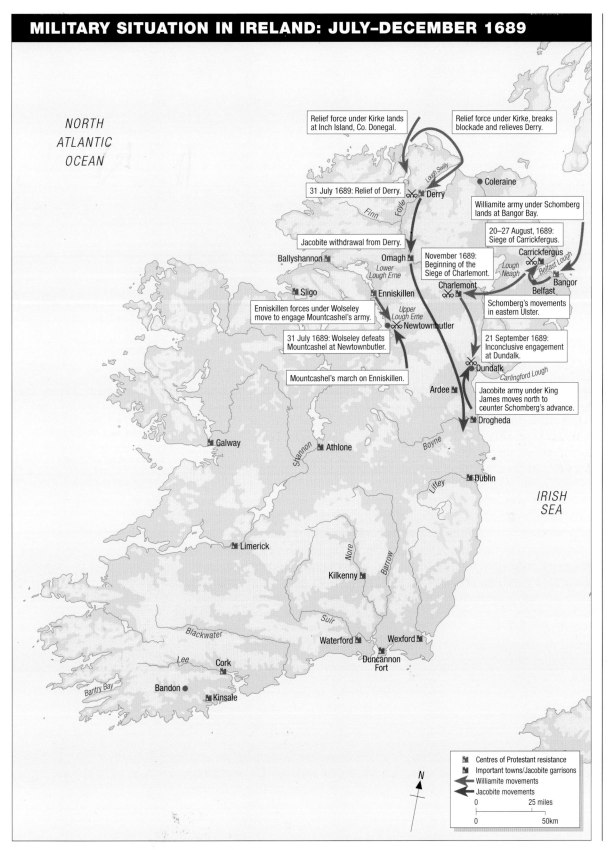

NORTH ATLANTIC OCEAN

Relief force under Kirke lands at Inch Island, Co. Donegal.

Relief force under Kirke, breaks blockade and relieves Derry.

● Coleraine

31 July 1689: Relief of Derry.

⚔ Derry

Lough Swilly

Foyle

Finn

Williamite army under Schomberg lands at Bangor Bay.

20–27 August, 1689: Siege of Carrickfergus.

Carrickfergus

Belfast Lough

Jacobite withdrawal from Derry.

Ballyshannon 🏰

Omagh 🏰

Lower Lough Erne

November 1689: Beginning of the Siege of Charlemont.

Lough Neagh

Bangor

🏰 Sligo

Charlemont ⚔

Belfast

Enniskillen forces under Wolseley move to engage Mountcashel's army.

🏰 Enniskillen

Upper Lough Erne

⚔ Newtownbutler

Schomberg's movements in eastern Ulster.

31 July 1689: Wolseley defeats Mountcashel at Newtownbutler.

21 September 1689: Inconclusive engagement at Dundalk.

⚔ Dundalk

Carlingford Lough

Mountcashel's march on Enniskillen.

Ardee 🏰

Jacobite army under King James moves north to counter Schomberg's advance.

● Drogheda

🏰 Galway

Shannon

🏰 Athlone

Boyne

Liffey

🏰 Dublin

IRISH SEA

🏰 Limerick

Nore

Barrow

Kilkenny 🏰

Suir

Blackwater

Waterford 🏰

Wexford 🏰

Lee

Cork 🏰

Duncannon Fort 🏰

Bantry Bay

Bandon ●

🏰 Kinsale

N

🏰 Centres of Protestant resistance
🏰 Important towns/Jacobite garrisons
← Williamite movements
← Jacobite movements

| 0 | 25 miles |
| 0 | 50km |

would offset his now critical lack of cavalry, Mountcashel deployed his few artillery pieces on the road, flanking them with infantry. Parties then went forward to raze the village and deny the enemy any cover. Moving through the town, Wolseley elected to immediately launch an attack, and, as his forces left the smoking ruins, they soon discovered that the warm weather had somewhat dried the marshy ground, making it firmer underfoot and thereby partially nullifying the defenders' advantage.

The Enniskillen infantry stormed along the causeway and, despite concentrated fire from the Jacobite foot, overran the enemy guns, giving Wolseley the opportunity to unleash his cavalry. The effect was electric: the Jacobite line began to waver and then broke in total panic. Mountcashel made a futile attempt to halt the tide, but it was to no avail and, severely wounded, he was taken prisoner.

Having beaten one enemy, Wolseley turned his troops about and force-marched them westwards to face Sarsfield, but military sense and orders from Dublin had instructed him to withdraw from the Erne Valley. Arriving at Enniskillen, Wolseley detached troops to reinforce Ballyshannon, and it was from here that a column was detached to find Sarsfield's army. Approaching Sligo from the south, a captured Jacobite straggler was sent into the town, spreading the rumour that the small Williamite force was the advance guard of a far larger army. As the misinformation spread, so did the size of the approaching force magnify. Panic set in and the defending soldiers, the majority of whom were irregulars, began to desert in significant numbers. Unable to stop the disintegration of his command, Sarsfield gathered what troops he could and withdrew to Athlone, leaving Sligo to the enemy.

From the heady days of spring, when it seemed as if King James's forces would carry all before them, the wheel had turned full circle. Hard on the heels of the setbacks in the west came further bad news for the Dublin government. On 27 July, Jacobite hopes in Scotland collapsed with the death of 'Bonnie Dundee' (John Graham, Viscount Dundee) at Killiecrankie, whilst on 18 August, after many delays, the Williamite army, which had been assembling near Hoylake in Cheshire, finally landed in Bangor Bay. The war for the crown of England would after all be fought in Ireland.

SCHOMBERG'S WAR

Once his position in England had been secured, William turned his eye to Ireland. Following the relief of Derry, the plan was quite simply to land an army of 22,000 men in Ireland and defeat the Jacobites in a single pitched battle. The simplest of plans often take the longest time to execute, and by mid-July the army was still forming around Chester.

William's first choice of commander for the expeditionary force was Friedrich Hermann, Duke of Schomberg, a 75-year-old veteran who had fought in most European wars of the preceding half-century, mainly for King Louis XIV of France, but who was currently in the service of William's cousin, the Elector of Brandenburg. The appointment of a foreigner to command an army for service in Ireland underlines William's understandably deep distrust of the English military hierarchy: officers such as John Churchill and Percy Kirke had turned their coats in his favour in 1688, and a Jacobite victory could easily induce them to renounce their new-found loyalty.

As to the composition of the army, William decided that it would be formed around a nucleus of veteran Dutch troops, bolstered by a number of newly raised regiments who would have no loyalty to the house of Stuart. To ensure this, Churchill, the newly created Earl of Marlborough, was sent to Flanders at the head of 7,000 English veterans, with a similar number of Dutch troops being transferred to William by the States General.

Eventually surmounting the problems caused by a rudimentary commissariat, Schomberg's leading elements landed in Bangor Bay on 13 August 1689 and, after the arrival of a second convoy, the army marched into Belfast four days later. In order to secure the countryside, Schomberg's first objective was to take the coastal town of Carrickfergus, which was held by a small Jacobite garrison who, with a siege inevitable, burnt the outlying suburbs and retired behind the walls.

On 20 August 1689, Schomberg placed Carrickfergus under siege and naval blockade, and for a week the town was bombarded from all sides. Initially terms were sought by the defenders, but they were refused and the Williamite guns continued to batter the defences until 27 August, when the garrison was granted the 'honours of war'. The next day, they marched out, but the sight of their enemy leaving with apparent impunity proved too much for some of the locals, and they attacked the Jacobite column – it was with difficulty that Schomberg was able to restore order, albeit at gunpoint.

King James's French advisors immediately counselled a withdrawal into the west of Ireland in order to draw out the campaign, but to James the road to Dublin was now open, and to him, possibly recalling his indecision the previous winter, Dublin *was* Ireland – therefore the capital had to be protected at all costs. The main body of the army moved north as far as Drogheda, and Berwick was detached with a column of troops to delay Schomberg's advance.

The young Duke began a systematic policy of destruction, burning Newry to the ground and damaging roads and bridges in order to impede the Williamite progress. Ordinarily, Berwick's actions might have been simply an inconvenience to the enemy, but, combined with the deteriorating weather, they soon became a major problem.

As Berwick's forces withdrew steadily in front of him, Schomberg pitched camp, a little to the north of Dundalk on 'a low, moist ground under great hills'. With the adverse weather, it is inconceivable that he could have chosen a worse site. Whereas the Dutch and French Huguenot units had all seen active service, the newly raised English units had not, and thus, while the veterans took measures to protect themselves from the appalling conditions, the Englishmen failed to do so. An epidemic of camp fever broke out – in all probability pneumonia – and the contagion spread like wildfire. The official death toll for the period September 1689–February 1690 was put at 5,674 men, almost one-third of the Williamite army.

Whilst the enemy suffered at Dundalk, James decided on a show of force and led his army from Drogheda northwards through Ardee, arriving before the Williamite encampment early on 21 September. Many of Schomberg's staff pressed him to order the attack, but he preferred to remain within his defences, and after some desultory fire the Jacobites retired, once more burning the countryside in their wake. To all intents and purposes the campaign was at an end, with both armies moving into winter quarters.

Despite the lack of a pitched battle, the Williamites had consolidated their position in Ulster and – with the exception of the fort at Charlemont – driven the Jacobites from the province. James therefore needed to regain some form of momentum, and whilst the main armies licked their wounds and began to prepare for the coming year's campaign, Patrick Sarsfield was sent west with a small force to retake Sligo and stabilize the situation in Connaught.

Lessons had been learnt from the earlier campaign, and coordinating his movements with local forces, Sarsfield reached Roscommon on 12 October. From here small parties were sent out to cover the advance, securing forage and supplies. Thomas Lloyd, commander of the Williamite forces in the region was unquestionably a gifted commander of irregular forces, but he was not defensively minded, and committed two grave errors which would have a severe impact on the coming operations. Firstly, he failed to ensure that the magazines at Sligo were adequately stocked, thereby reducing the likelihood of the town being able to withstand a prolonged siege, and secondly, he reverted to the role of 'independent commander of cavalry', leading a force out from Sligo to engage Jacobite foragers but being ambushed whilst crossing the Curlew Mountains.

Other attempts to halt the Jacobite advance met with similar failure. Soon Sarsfield had reached the small village of Ballysadare where, having destroyed the bridge, Lloyd's forces attempted once more to frustrate the enemy's plans. Whilst his artillery bombarded Lloyd's positions, Sarsfield sent a mixed force under Henry Luttrell to cross the river and outflank the enemy. Outpacing his dragoons and infantry, Luttrell soon found himself sandwiched between Lloyd's forces and some reinforcements. With few options available to him, Luttrell formed his men and charged the newly arrived troopers, scattering them. As the remainder of the flanking force came up, Lloyd, realizing that his position was by now untenable, withdrew once more to Sligo. However, as the Jacobite army continued to advance, Lloyd decided to cut his way out, leaving a battalion of Huguenot troops under the command of Colonel St Sauveur to hold the town.

Considerably outnumbering the defenders, Sarsfield decided to conduct a conventional siege. However, it soon became apparent that his field artillery was insufficient to breach the walls, and, unsure of how well provided the garrison was, he opted for the unconventional and ordered his engineers to construct a *sow*, a form of medieval siege tower, which would enable his men to drop onto the town's ramparts and seize the town that way. The Frenchmen manning the walls may have been surprised by the engine, but were most certainly not overawed: as it was wheeled towards the walls they opened up with a fierce fire, eventually destroying the device.

Frustrated, Sarsfield settled down to starve the defenders out, but on the third day of the siege and unaware of Lloyd's failure to adequately provision Sligo, he summoned the town to surrender. It must have come as both a shock and relief to him when his terms were accepted, with the defenders being granted safe conduct to Ballyshannon. Before returning to Dublin, Sarsfield detached a sizeable garrison under Henry Luttrell, with orders to expand and improve the defences during the winter to ensure that Sligo remain in Jacobite hands.

As both armies went into cantonments in preparation for the coming campaigning season, their respective approaches to the situation could not have been more different: Schomberg, for his part, attempted to resolve the problems that had plagued him in 1689, firstly by reorganizing his forces in an attempt to make good the army's losses in men and equipment, and secondly by overhauling his commissariat – 2,500 horses, 100 artillery wagons and 450 transport wagons arrived in Ireland, and, although they eased Schomberg's transport problems, they would soon cause problems of their own: whilst marching through hostile country they would need to carry their own supplies and thus their usefulness to the army would be that much reduced.

Plans were laid for a drive on Dublin, from which point future strategy would be decided; with the capture of the Irish capital, communications with England would be that much more secure and the transfer of troops and supplies made that much easier.

For their part, the Jacobites appeared to have fallen into a state of overconfidence – claiming Schomberg's refusal to give battle as a moral victory. Many officers left their regiments to attend to their personal affairs, and therefore, at a time when the army should have been reorganizing itself for the coming campaign, many of its leaders were absent, albeit with leave; indeed, this state of affairs began to filter down to the rank and file, with many regiments being able to muster only a fraction of their authorized strength.

Although he was with the army, James avoided any pretence at command and moved his headquarters from Dublin to Kilkenny, allegedly to escape an epidemic similar to that which had laid Schomberg's troops low. Here he displayed a worrying lack of knowledge of the realities of his situation, confidently writing to his Scottish supporters that the Duke of Berwick would lead an army of

8,000 troops to their assistance in the spring of 1690. Exactly how this was to be achieved in the face of overwhelming English naval superiority and without the commitment of the French fleet was never explained.

In Dublin Castle, Tyrconnel saw the situation with great clarity: William's regime was unpopular, and with continued French assistance once Ireland had been secured, England would fall into James's hands like a ripe plum. He saw correctly, however, that this discontent was a transitory thing and that if William was given time 'he will by all sorts of wayes and meanes establish his tyranny over these helpless people in one year's time more'.

At Versailles, Tyrconnel's pleas were heard sympathetically by Louis XIV who sincerely wanted to help his cousin James but only so far as it coincided with his own strategic plans: the continuation of the conflict in Ireland was desirable if only because it kept William III's attention focused firmly away from Flanders which, for Louis, was the main theatre of war.

Accordingly, a major convoy under the Marquis d'Amfreville sailed from Brest on 17 March 1690: aboard were the Comte de Lauzun and a brigade of over 6,000 French infantry and a number of individual officers – gunners, commissaries, artisans, engineers and surgeons – on attachment to the Jacobite army. De Lauzun's forces were an invaluable reinforcement for James, but it was to be a poisoned chalice as, in return, Louis expected the transfer of an equal number of Irish troops to serve in the French army under the command of Mountcashel. The convoy also brought over 1,000,000lb of much needed military supplies, ranging from uniforms, arms and ammunition to foodstuffs.

The fleet arrived at Cork on 22 March and departed on 18 April for Brest, carrying on board Mountcashel and five regiments of Irish foot. Also aboard were the French ambassador, d'Avaux, and Marshal de Rosen, neither of whose departure was viewed as a serious loss by King James. To him, one was simply a French spy whose advice could not be relied upon, whilst the other was a barbarian, as exemplified by his conduct during the siege of Derry.

A CHALLENGE ACCEPTED

Not surprisingly, the view from London was slightly different. In October 1689, William had successfully persuaded parliament to vote on the allocation of funds for the continuation of hostilities, and a sum of two million pounds sterling was agreed upon, not just for the maintenance of Schomberg's army but also for that of the Royal Navy and Marlborough's forces in Flanders. Armed with these monies, William was also able to raise several new regiments and to conclude the hiring of a contingent of troops from Denmark.

Despite these preparations, William was painfully aware of the fragility of his government's position and acknowledged the fact that whilst James was able to rule unchallenged from Dublin, his own position would never be truly secure: although a Protestant and therefore acceptable to the majority of the population, he was in the final analysis not an Englishman, and this counted badly against him, especially as many who had supported his invasion and accession with the anticipation of future

favours had yet to receive them, all the while watching as his Dutch advisors received preferment and advancement. The answer was simple: he must travel to Ireland and assume command, defeating James before his father-in-law could transfer a significant force to either England or Scotland: God himself would either endorse or refute his claim on the field of battle. His decision was not, as has often been viewed, a reflection of his opinion of the handling of the 1689 campaign; there were several very experienced commanders available to William should he have simply wished to replace Schomberg. To quieten his domestic opponents he had to win the war, win it quickly and above all win it convincingly, in order to unite the country against the real enemy, France.

Accordingly, he addressed both Houses of Parliament on 27 January 1690, confirming his intention to travel to Ireland in order to bring the war to a final conclusion, adding, 'It is a very sensible affliction to me, to see my good people burthened with taxes; but, since the speedy recovery of Ireland is, in my opinion, the only means to ease them, and to preserve the peace and honour of the nation, I am resolved to go thither in person.' Not surprisingly parliament assented to the King's request, but with commitments to England's allies, it would take several months before William was ready to sail for Ireland.

THE SUMMER OF 1690

As the weather began to improve, both sides began to call in their detachments from their winter cantonments, in order to concentrate their forces for the decisive encounter that both commanders sought: Schomberg needed to break out of Ulster and destroy James's army before reducing any Jacobite garrisons, whilst, for his part, James needed to either defeat Schomberg decisively or at least keep him penned up in the north so that forces could be transferred to either England or Scotland to unite with his supporters there.

Schomberg moved first, and at the beginning of May 1690 his forces struck southwards towards the enemy fort at Charlemont, situated on the main highway between Armagh and Dungannon. The works were well sited, overlooking the river Blackwater, and partially protected from attack by a bog on their southern approaches, being held by upwards of 800 Jacobite troops under the command of Colonel Teague O'Regan. As the enemy noose began to tighten, O'Regan received an unlooked-for reinforcement of 500 men, which became more of a liability than an asset as the troops placed a heavy strain on his already acute supply problems.

On 12 May, the garrison agreed to accept terms, and his troops marched out to join the Jacobite forces at Dundalk, where O'Regan was knighted by a grateful King James. At roughly the same time, Colonel Wolseley, operating out of Enniskillen, captured the enemy position at Ballynacarraig in County Cavan. Apart from a few isolated enemy garrisons, which could be masked and allowed to wither on the vine, the north had been swept clear of Jacobite forces.

The 'escape' of King William. Wounded on the eve of the battle by Jacobite artillery fire, William would have several further brushes with death during the confused fighting around Donore and Platin Hall. (With kind permission of the Trustees, Atlas Van Stolk, Rotterdam)

The opinion in the Jacobite camp was that the Williamite army had two options when it advanced out of Ulster. The first was to move southeastwards from Cavan whilst the second was for it to move along the east coast through Newry and thence via the Moyry Pass to Dundalk, less than 50 miles from Dublin. Accordingly, King James deployed the bulk of his army in forward positions, covering Trim, Kells and Ardee, whilst detachments under the Frenchman Léry, Marquis de Girardin, and Colonel Sarsfield were sent to occupy Dundalk, and the village of Finea, in County Cavan, respectively.

Schomberg was not destined to redeem himself in the eyes of his detractors as, on 14 June 1690, William landed at Carrickfergus at the head of 15,000 reinforcements for the army in Ireland. Local enthusiasm for William soared as the Dutch and Danish veterans trooped off the transports, a wave of confidence beginning to grow, for although William did not have a spectacular record as a field commander, many were aware of the fact that he rarely acted unless he felt himself to be in an advantageous position.

William's proposed strategy was simple: trusting in what he believed to be his numerical and qualitative superiority, he would drive southwards via Newry and the Moyry Pass, with his final objective being the capture of Dublin. As it was inconceivable that James would give up his capital without a fight, he would meet and defeat the Jacobite army en route. He therefore issued instructions that the army would concentrate at Loughbrickland in County Down.

As soon as word reached James that the Williamites had vacated western Ulster, he resolved to advance to the southern entrance to the Moyry Pass and engage the enemy there, at a location which would nullify their superior numbers. The pass was well known in Irish history, for it was here at the 'Gap of the North' that the legendary warrior Cuchullain had defended Ulster against an army commanded by Queen Maeve of Connaught.

Whilst the Jacobites could most certainly have bottled up the Williamites in the pass, de Lauzun, commander of the French brigade and a personal friend of James, suggested that the position was not only too far advanced from the magazine at Dublin, but also that it could easily be outflanked from Armagh. It had the makings of another legendary defence: Thermopylae.

Taking de Lauzun's advice, James ordered the army to march south, leaving a mixed force of infantry and cavalry under Lieutenant Colonel Laurence Dempsey of Galmoy's Regiment of Horse to ambush William's leading elements as they advanced through the pass. The Irishmen sprang their ambush too soon, and, although both sides claimed to have inflicted more damage on their opponents, it is generally accepted that the Jacobites had had the upper hand. The victory was a pyrrhic one, however, as Dempsey, one of James's most experienced officers was mortally wounded, dying at Oldbridge a few days later.

The failure to hold the entrance to the Moyry Pass has been cited as the turning point of the war, especially by several officers in the Jacobite army who were writing to explain the defeat at the Boyne. Although de Lauzun's advice to James must always be seen in the light of his own instructions from Versailles not to unnecessarily jeopardize the French brigade, he was probably correct in his assumption: William's army would most certainly have been bloodied as it advanced through the pass, but should a successful envelopment have been attempted, James simply didn't have enough troops to both hold Moyry and defeat the flank move simultaneously, as at this time, with detachments still en route from outlying garrisons, his forces were in all probability outnumbered by almost two to one.

The real significance of James's decision to accept de Lauzun's counsel and withdraw from Dundalk/Moyry is that it left a single natural obstacle that would facilitate a defence being mounted north of Dublin – the Boyne.

THE EVE OF BATTLE

On 29 June 1690, King James's army crossed the Boyne at Drogheda and Oldbridge, and encamped on the northern slopes of the Hill of Donore. Knowing that the Williamite army was little more than a day behind, the army began to deploy defensively: Brian Magennis, Viscount Iveagh, was ordered to fortify Drogheda with three regiments of foot – a little over 1,300 men – and hold the bridge there, whilst Richard Bourke, Earl of Clanrickarde, was to occupy the village of Oldbridge and prepare it for defence. Finally, and in order to channel the enemy forces, a detachment was sent to destroy the bridge at Slane, several miles upstream. Late on the 29th, King James's army was bolstered by the arrival of 3,000 men under Patrick Sarsfield, who had marched from County Cavan when the Williamite forces opposing them had moved east to join their main army at Loughbrickland.

During the morning of Monday, 30 June, the leading elements of William's forces began to arrive in the hills overlooking the northern bank of the Boyne, with the king himself arriving a little after 9.00am, establishing his command post in the ruins of Mellifont Abbey. A party under Captain Pownel of Leveson's dragoons was sent towards Slane to ascertain the condition of the bridge there, whilst further detachments were sent down to the river to probe the Jacobite defences around Oldbridge, immediately coming under artillery and small-arms fire from the positions on the southern bank.

Despite the fact that his own artillery was still on the march from Dundalk, William then sent a mixed force of horse and dragoons – including his own *Gardes te Paard* – to reconnoitre the riverbank. Again the Irish troops opened fire, causing a significant number of casualties: the Dutch Horse Guards lost some 20 men, about 8 per cent of their regimental strength, before William gave permission for the horsemen to withdraw to cover. It was a costly way in which to scout the Jacobite positions, and two contemporary theories were put forward as the reasons behind William's actions: firstly, that he wanted to see how well his troops would stand under fire, a view which does not hold up to scrutiny, as a large number of the troops involved belonged to his own Guards Regiment, and thus were assumed to be the steadiest troops in the army. The second theory, as put forward by Jacob Hop, envoy of the Dutch States General, is that William wanted to provoke the Jacobites into attacking and thereby bring on a major engagement. Exactly why William would choose to do this without adequate intelligence of enemy numbers and deployments, and especially when his own army was still not fully deployed, is unclear.

Not satisfied with the results of either of these reconnaissances, William, accompanied by his staff, rode down towards the river where they studied Oldbridge for a while before riding eastwards a short distance where they dismounted in full view of the Jacobite army and began to have lunch. A party of Jacobite horse – reputedly including Tyrconnel, Berwick, Sarsfield, de Lauzun and Parker amongst their number – then rode down towards the river opposite William's entourage. Two small cannon were brought up and, as William and his aides mounted, they opened fire: the first shot exploded amongst the staff, killing one man and several horses, but the second took a cruel deflection and, bouncing off the ground, struck William in the shoulder. The horsemen closed ranks, and rode back to headquarters in order to have the King examined by his physician. Rumours of William's death immediately began to circulate in both camps; the report quickly reached Paris, where the guns of the Bastille fired a *feu de joie* and where the mob celebrated by burning effigies of William and his queen, Mary, even attempting to light bonfires in the courtyard of the Palace of Versailles.

Once his wound had been dressed, and in order to allay any fears about to his health, William elected to ride around the camp in the company of the Duke of Schomberg, to the cheers and acclamation of the entire army and, on his return to his headquarters at Mellifont Abbey, he summoned his senior officers to a council of war to take place later that evening. Whatever the expectations of either James or William, one thing was certain: that a battle would be fought the following morning and that it would have a decisive effect on the war for Ireland, and ultimately the war for the throne of England.

CHRONOLOGY

1633   Birth of James Stuart, Duke of York.

1642   Outbreak of the English Civil War.

1649   Execution of King Charles I. End of the English Civil War.

1648   Duke of York escapes from parliamentary custody and goes into exile.

1650   Beginning of York's service in the French army under Turenne.

1656   Anglo-French treaty compels Duke of York to resign from French army. Takes service with the Spanish armed forces.

1658   Anglo-French army defeats Spanish at the battle of the Dunes.

1660   Restoration of King Charles II.

1672   William of Orange appointed Stadtholder of Holland and Captain-General of Dutch Republic.

1677   William of Orange marries Mary, eldest daughter of James, Duke of York.

1685   6 February – Death of King Charles II of England, accession of James II.

11 June – Duke of Monmouth lands at Lyme Regis in Dorset.

20 June – Richard Talbot appointed Earl of Tyrconnel.

6 July – Defeat of Monmouth's forces at the battle of Sedgemoor.

15 July – Monmouth executed in London.

1686   Formation of the League of Augsburg, a Dutch-sponsored anti-French alliance.

Earl of Clarendon sworn in as Lord Lieutenant of Ireland.

Tyrconnel appointed Marshal of Ireland, Commander-in-Chief of Irish army.

1687   Clarendon recalled and Tyrconnel appointed Lord Deputy in his stead.

1688   10 June – Birth of James Francis Edward, Prince of Wales.

1 November – William of Orange's invasion force sails from the Netherlands.

5 November – William of Orange lands at Torbay in Devon.

23 November – Mountjoy's regiment withdrawn from Derry, leaving city ungarrisoned.

24 November – John Churchill leads desertion of King James's senior officers.

7 December – Gates of Derry are closed to Antrim's regiment.

11 December – James II's attempted flight to France ends in capture.

18 December – William of Orange enters London, de facto King of England.

23 December – James II successfully flees to France.

1689   8 January – William of Orange sends Richard Hamilton to Dublin to negotiate with Tyrconnel.

29 January – Tyrconnel begins expansion of Irish army.

13 February – William and Mary accept Bill of Rights and are crowned joint sovereigns.

7 March – Tyrconnel offers conditional pardon to Protestant Associations then under arms.

12 March – James II lands at Kinsale, County Cork.

14 March – Richard Hamilton defeats Ulster Protestants at Dromore, County Down.

27 March – Richard Hamilton summons Coleraine to surrender.

7 April – Jacobite forces successfully cross the river Bann at Portglenone.

14 April – Derry garrison sorties out, but is defeated by the Jacobites at Cladyford.

18 April – James II refused entry into Derry, siege of city begins in earnest.

21 April – Death of the French General de Maumont during fighting at Pennyburn Mill.

1 May – Anglo-French fleets fight inconclusive battle in Bantry Bay.

22 June – James's parliament in Dublin repeals Restoration Land Settlement.

28 June – Clancarty's regiment launches last major attack on Derry's defences.

27 July – Jacobites victorious at Killiecrankie in Scotland, their commander Dundee is mortally wounded.

28 July – Williamite ships break boom across the Foyle and relieve Derry.

31 July – Jacobite army defeated by Enniskillen forces at Newtownbutler, County Fermanagh.

31 July – Hamilton withdraws from Derry, siege ends after 105 days.

13 August – Initial elements of Schomberg's army land in Bangor Bay.

27 August – After a week-long siege, Jacobite garrison of Carrickfergus capitulates.

1690 18 April – 'Mountcashel Brigade' leaves Ireland to enter French service.

14 June – Jacobite garrison of Charlemont surrenders to Schomberg's forces.

14 June – William III lands at Carrickfergus with 15,000 additional troops.

30 June – French naval victory over Anglo-Dutch fleet off Beachy Head.

1 July – William III victorious over James II at the Boyne.

4 July – James II sails to France from Kinsale.

6 July – William III enters Dublin.

17–24 July – Unsuccessful Williamite siege of Athlone.

9–30 August – Unsuccessful Williamite siege of Limerick.

5 September – William III returns to England, appoints Ginkel as army commander.

12 September – Tyrconnel sails to France accompanied by de Lauzun and the French brigade.

28 September – John Churchill, Earl of Marlborough, captures strategic port of Cork.

1691 14 January – Tyrconnel returns to Ireland.

9 May – The French general St Ruth appointed to command Jacobite army.

21–30 June – Ginkel successfully besieges and takes Athlone.

12 July – Jacobites decisively defeated at Aughrim, County Galway.

21 July – Ginkel captures Galway.

25 August – Williamites under Ginkel besiege Limerick for the second time.

14 September – Sligo surrenders to the Williamites.

3 October – Treaty of Limerick is signed, effectively ending the war in Ireland.

22 December – 12,000 troops under Sarsfield sail to France to take service under James II.

OPPOSING COMMANDERS

THE JACOBITES

King James II of England and Ireland, VII of Scotland (1633–1701)

The second son of King Charles I, James, Duke of York had never really expected to succeed to the throne of England. Deeply scarred by his father's execution, he spent his years of exile in the service of both France and Spain, earning a reputation that belied his actions in later years. No less a soldier than Turenne, France's premier general, would mention the Duke several times in despatches, praising his gallantry and courage under fire.

In 1660, the Stuart monarchy was restored and the Duke of York reappointed as Lord High Admiral, tasked with creating a force that would be able to meet England's enemies on equal terms. In partnership with the Secretary of the Navy, Samuel Pepys, he did just this, laying the foundations of the Royal Navy, which would ensure British naval supremacy throughout the 18th and 19th centuries.

Following the inconclusive and controversial victory at Sole Bay on 13 June 1665, James was forcibly retired from active service and it was shortly after this that he fatally showed his political inexperience in openly acknowledging his conversion to Roman Catholicism. In 1671, the recently widowed James married Mary-Beatrice d'Este, daughter of the Duke of Modena. Again his enemies took note and attempted to have James disbarred from the succession on the death of Charles II, with the crown passing to his eldest daughter Mary.

In 1677, and against her father's wishes, the Princess Mary married her cousin, William-Henry van Nassau, Stadtholder of the United Dutch Provinces and hereditary Prince of Orange. Despite the marriage, and ignoring pressure from sections of parliament, Charles II refused to remove his brother as heir apparent, and upon Charles's death in 1685 James became king.

The outset of King James II's relatively short reign began auspiciously enough with the resolution of the Crown Debt and the securing of future revenues, but with the Argyll and Monmouth rebellions, public opinion began to turn against him. This, coupled with his ill-advised and disastrous policies on religious freedom, made it easy for his domestic enemies to fully discredit and undermine him, leading to the events of 1688.

Following the failure of his Irish campaign, James went into exile for a final time, eventually seeing the chances of a second Restoration being dashed by the victory of the Anglo-Dutch over the French at the battle of Barfleur/La Hogue on 29 May 1692.

For the remainder of his life he remained the focus of the Jacobite court in exile at the palace of St Germains-en-Laye, just outside Paris, where, after suffering a stroke, he died on 2 September 1701, aged 68.

King James II. Inflexible and wilful, James came late in life to the throne and was unsuited to the role of king. His indecision would cost him the throne in 1688, and his intractability would cost him the chance of regaining it two years later. (With kind permission of the Trustees, National Portrait Gallery, London)

Richard Talbot, Earl and Duke of Tyrconnel. Although later castigated by his peers, without Tyrconnel's personality and ability the Jacobite cause in Ireland would have been stillborn. While James vacillated, he persuaded Louis XIV of France that a second Stuart Restoration, based in Ireland, could succeed. (With kind permission of the Trustees, National Portrait Gallery, London)

Richard Talbot, Earl and titular Duke of Tyrconnel (c.1630–1691)

Talbot first came to prominence during the English Civil War when, in 1649, he was one of the few survivors of Cromwell's sack of Drogheda. Fleeing Ireland he joined the Stuart court in exile, and tested his luck once more when he was part of a failed plot to assassinate Cromwell, managing to escape from custody the night before he was due to be sent to the Tower of London to be executed.

Following his escape, Talbot then hitched his star to James, Duke of York, and after the Restoration returned to London where he began to dabble in politics. During the next few years his activities were rewarded with short stays in the Tower of London, and, following the death of his first wife, he married Frances Hamilton (née Jennings), thereby becoming brother-in-law to Sir John Churchill, future Earl and Duke of Marlborough.

In May 1685, Talbot was raised to the Irish peerage as Earl of Tyrconnel, the title by which he is generally known, and later that year was authorized by the crown to begin the reorganization of the army in Ireland. Initially he began to disarm the Protestant militia but then, as his position over the army was made secure against the Earl of Clarendon, James's Lord Lieutenant in Ireland, he began to replace Protestant army officers with Catholic ones, creating an Anglo-Irish officer corps who were dependent on him alone for favour and advancement.

Following the events of 1688, he once more expanded the Irish army, bringing it to a paper strength of around 50,000 men, and it was this force that persuaded both King James and King Louis XIV of France of the feasibility of a second Stuart Restoration taking place from Ireland. For the next two years Tyrconnel schemed and manipulated affairs, emerging as the pivotal figure in Ireland without whom neither James nor William, nor even Louis XIV of France would be able to realize their plans.

In failing health, Tyrconnel would dominate King James's councils until the Boyne, but following the King's flight, his influence waned owing to the emergence of other Irish leaders such as Patrick Sarsfield. On 14 August 1691, he died of a stroke at Limerick.

James Fitzjames, Duke of Berwick (1670–1734)

The eldest son of James, Duke of York, and Arabella Churchill, Berwick was the youngest cavalry general of his day. Despite his youth, he was a veteran soldier by the time he arrived in Ireland, having served in the Imperial army, taking part in the capture of Buda in 1686 and serving on the Drave the following year.

Following the conclusion of the campaign in Hungary, Berwick returned to England, being appointed governor of Portsmouth and colonel of the Royal Horse Guards. Although appointed to command the royal forces at Salisbury in 1688, he was unable to prevent the defection of several senior officers to William of Orange, and soon joined the Jacobite exodus to the Continent.

In February 1689, Berwick came to Ireland as part of his father's suite and was appointed to the command of the second troop of Life Guards. Under Hamilton, he took part in the initial battles in Ulster, and whilst Hamilton oversaw the siege of Derry, Berwick was employed in punitive actions against Williamite enclaves in the north-west, a role which prepared him for the 'scorched earth' tactics of early 1690.

At the Boyne he was in effective command of both troops of Life Guards and, despite his youth, led them in several charges that helped to stabilize the precarious Jacobite position and allowed the army to withdraw in some semblance of order.

Following King James's flight from Ireland, Berwick acted as viceroy in his father's name until his recall in January 1691, eventually adopting French nationality and accepting a general's commission from King Louis XIV. Berwick spent the rest of his life in French service, being killed at the battle of Philippsburg in 1734.

Lieutenant General Richard Hamilton (??–1717)

The fifth son of Sir George and Lady Mary Hamilton of Roscrea, Richard Hamilton followed family tradition by enlisting in King Charles II's Life Guards at an early age, but transferred to his brother's regiment in the French army when political pressure led to the exclusion of Catholics from public or military office. When the political climate changed, he returned to English service.

Sent to England at the head of his regiment in 1687, he was interned on the Isle of Wight in 1688 and, through his family connections, both Catholic and Protestant, was recommended to William III as a suitable envoy to convince Tyrconnel to come to terms with the new regime.

Hamilton lost no time in pursuing the opposite course, helping to persuade the Lord Deputy to maintain his loyalty to James, and was rewarded with a lieutenant general's commission. Placed in command of a small Jacobite army, a series of workmanlike victories enabled Hamilton to clear most of Ulster of Williamite enclaves – reducing them to just Derry and Enniskillen – but was thwarted in his attempt to negotiate the surrender of the former, the failure of which acted as a springboard for the Williamite campaign of 1690.

At the Boyne, he commanded a brigade of foot at the crucial Oldbridge sector, and following the Jacobite collapse led a delaying action which, although resulting in his capture, allowed a large number of Jacobite troops to escape the field.

After the war he was exchanged for Lord Mountjoy and was a senior figure in the Jacobite high command during the failed invasion attempts of 1692, 1696 and 1708.

Antonin Nompar de Caumont, Comte (later Duc) de Lauzun (1632–1723)

A 'career socialite', de Lauzun's credentials for the command of the French forces in Ireland lay not with any proven or innate military ability, but simply in the fact that he had helped to escort Queen Mary-Beatrice to France in 1688. This dubious qualification was reinforced by the fact that he had earlier been imprisoned in the fortress of Pignerol following an affair with the sister of King Louis XIV, and he was under no illusions with regards to his fate should he not obey to the letter his orders not to take any unnecessary risks with the troops under his command.

De Lauzun's record in Ireland is at first glance a bad one. At the Boyne, he overreacted to the Williamite flanking manoeuvre and issued the orders which led to the majority of the Jacobite army moving away from the crucial sector and effectively condemning Tyrconnel to defeat.

Antonin Nompar de Caumont, Comte et Duc de Lauzun. Awarded the Order of the Garter for his services in aiding the Queen's escape from England in 1688, de Lauzun's appointment to command the French forces in Ireland was a political sinecure rather than a military appointment. (Art Resource Inc, New York)

King William III. Charismatic and displaying inspirational leadership in the field, William won his victory at the Boyne, but the price was to lose the chance of securing peace. Following the Finglas Declaration, the war would drag on for another year. (Photograph courtesy of the National Gallery of Ireland, Dublin)

Friedrich Hermann, 1st Duke of Schomberg. Probably the most famous soldier of his day, Schomberg's initial campaign was dogged by failure. Despite his misgivings about the plan, he led the Williamite centre at the Boyne, falling at the head of Caillemotte's Battalion as it was attacked by the Jacobite horse. (With kind permission of the Trustees, National Portrait Gallery, London)

What must be balanced against this is the fact that he was instrumental in leading the bulk of the army off the field in relatively good order, thereby ensuring that the retreat did not become a rout.

Following the Jacobite withdrawal over the Shannon, de Lauzun led the French troops to garrison the city of Galway, from where they sailed to France in September 1690.

THE WILLIAMITES

William III, Prince of Orange, Stadtholder of the United Dutch Provinces, King of England (1650–1702)

Born a few weeks after his father's death, William's early life was one of obscurity. However, in 1672, and in response to the French invasion, the existing Dutch government was overthrown and William appointed Stadtholder, Captain-General and Admiral for life.

Undeterred by the enemy's superiority, William began to fight back, firstly securing a peace with France's English allies in 1674, and finally with France herself in 1678. The settlement with England strengthened William's position: it led in 1677 to his marriage with his cousin Mary, daughter of James, Duke of York, and niece of King Charles II.

Once peace had been signed with France, William embarked on what was to become the central theme of his adult life – the containment of France – and began to build up an anti-French coalition from amongst Louis XIV's many enemies.

Following Monmouth's execution in 1685, William became the obvious focus for dissidents within the English establishment, being invited in 1688 to invade the country and seize the throne in his wife's name. His sponsors were soon shown his mettle when they were informed that he would rule as a 'joint monarch' or not at all.

With one eye firmly on Flanders, Schomberg's failure to defeat King James in the field persuaded William that he would have to go to Ireland and finish things in person. Having secured an unprecedented amount of support from parliament, the army in Ireland was heavily reinforced and a decisive engagement sought.

The Boyne was not the climactic victory that had been anticipated and, in the wake of French victories at Beachy Head and Fleurus, the succeeding weeks were spent subduing the southern ports before William was again in a position to meet the Jacobite army, which was by now sheltering behind the walls of Limerick.

A combination of bad weather allied with a steadfast defence by the garrison denied William a second victory in Ireland and an early end to the war. As he returned to England in September 1690, both sides began to make ready to go into winter quarters in preparation for the resumption of hostilities the following year.

Friedrich Hermann, Duke of Schomberg (1615–1690)

After prior service in the Dutch and Swedish armies, Schomberg entered the French army in 1635, initially serving under Turenne. He was sent to Lisbon in 1659 at the request of King Charles II of England as a military advisor to assist the Portuguese in their war against Spain. Created Count of Mertola in 1663, he led the Portuguese to victory at the battle of Montes Claros in June 1665, and following the end of the war in Iberia returned to France, adopting French citizenship and receiving a promotion to lieutenant general.

Groomed for senior command, he narrowly missed an appointment as general-in-chief of the English army when popular pressure forced King Charles II to rescind his offer of employment. In 1675 he completed a series of successful operations in Catalonia and, following the capture of Bellegarde, received a marshal's baton. His elevation to the marshalate marked the high point of Schomberg's service to King Louis, and following the revocation of the Edict of Nantes in 1685, he left France to take up service with the Elector of Brandenburg, as general-in-chief of the Brandenburg army.

In 1688, and with the Elector's consent, Schomberg accepted a position as second in command to William of Orange in his invasion of England, and the following year led an expeditionary force into Ireland. A desultory campaign followed, in which a cautious policy resulted in severe losses through disease, and an impasse, which was only relieved by William's arrival in Ireland in 1690.

At the Boyne, Schomberg's cautious and methodical nature came to the fore when he proposed an indirect, flanking move as being the best option to guarantee success, but following William's rejection of the plan he was given command of the Williamite centre where he was killed whilst leading his troops into action to the east of Oldbridge.

Following the battle, the Duke was buried on the battlefield but was later re-interred in St Patrick's Cathedral in Dublin.

Meinhard, Count Schomberg, 1st Duke of Leinster, 3rd Duke of Schomberg (1641–1719)

The second son of Marshal Schomberg, Meinhard began his early military service in the French army, and following the revocation of the Edict of Nantes, he too transferred to the Brandenburg army, where he was eventually promoted to General der Kavallerie.

In March 1689, he joined the English army as an aide to King William, and as such acted as liaison between Whitehall and the army in Ireland, continuing with these duties until April 1690 when he was appointed colonel of the Duke of Devonshire's Regiment of Horse. This led to some confusion in the army rolls, as there were now two 'Schomberg's Horse', the former comprising French exiles, whilst the latter consisted of Englishmen.

Count Schomberg barely had time to adjust to his new rank: scarcely a week later, he was again promoted, this time to lieutenant general of horse, and given command of the cavalry element of the new expeditionary force that was being raised for service in Ireland.

On the morning of 1 July, he was detached with the right-wing cavalry, and Trelawney's brigade of foot to turn the Jacobite left flank and force a crossing of the Boyne. Although unable to close with the enemy, he drew off enough of King James's strength to fatally weaken the Oldbridge sector and virtually ensure the Williamite victory.

Schomberg served consistently throughout the rest of the war, adopting English citizenship and being created 1st Duke of Leinster in 1692. In 1693, following the death of his brother Karl at the battle of the Marsaglia, he became 3rd Duke of Schomberg.

Ferdinand-Wilhelm, Duke of Württemberg-Neustadt (1659–1701)

A contemporary of the Duke of Berwick, Württemberg entered the service of the Danish crown shortly after his 16th birthday, and after several years' distinguished service was promoted to lieutenant general at the age of 23. The following year he participated in the relief of Vienna and fought in the campaign to liberate Austria and Hungary from the Turks, suffering a severe head wound in 1685.

Following his recovery, Württemberg was recalled to Denmark where he was eventually given command of the forces hired by King William which, at the Boyne, finally snapped the over-extended Jacobite line.

Having participated in all the major engagements of the war in Ireland, Württemberg transferred to Flanders where the Danish contingent again distinguished itself, with the Duke eventually being made governor of 'Dutch Flanders'.

After the Treaty of Ryswick, he served against the Turks and the Swedes before returning to the Low Countries, where in 1701 he succumbed to ill health caused by his head wound of 16 years earlier.

Heinrich Traiectinus, Count Solms-Braunfels (1638–1693)

Solms was born in Utrecht in 1638, the son of Johann Albrecht von Solms-Braunfels, a German soldier in Dutch service, who was from 1644 until his death in 1648 Master-General of the Artillery of the United Dutch Provinces.

Receiving an honorary colonelcy of a Guelderland regiment in 1646, Solms's progress through the ranks was cemented not only by his late father's influence, but also by the fact that his aunt, Amalia, had married Frederick-Henry of Orange-Nassau, Stadtholder of the United Dutch Provinces in 1625, and thus was related to the Dutch ruling house.

Solms commanded an infantry regiment in 1667 following the outbreak of hostilities with France, transferring to the cavalry the following year, and then returning to the infantry in 1672, when he was promoted to major general. By 1674, his regiment was absorbed into the *Gardes te Voet* of which he was appointed colonel the following year, simultaneously being appointed governor of Nijmegen. In 1676 he was appointed as *bailli* of the Commandery of the Teutonic Knights at Utrecht (a position which he held until his death).

In 1683, Solms was promoted to lieutenant general of infantry, and took an active part in the planning of the expedition in 1688, being the first officer to land at Torbay. He was known for his distrust of William's newly acquired English supporters, and no doubt this opinion came across in Council, especially as William was habitually predisposed to the advice of his Dutch officers, particularly those with blood ties. Following James's successful flight, William appointed Solms as 'general over all Our foot forces' in the English army.

Upon his arrival in Ireland Solms's low opinion of the English was transferred to the new enemy, and accordingly he advocated a simple 'steamroller' attack at Oldbridge on 1 July 1690, preferring the direct approach as opposed to Schomberg's subtlety.

Following the Boyne, Solms remained at William's side, returning to England with him after the first siege of Limerick, and in 1691 he was promoted to full general in the Dutch army. He was killed in action in July 1693 during the Neerwinden campaign.

THE OPPOSING ARMIES

THE JACOBITE FORCES

Given the lack of accurate records, estimates of the size of King James's army at the Boyne vary greatly. However, most authorities tend to agree that it was about two-thirds the size of the Williamite army and would therefore have numbered something in the region of 24,000 men.

The army itself was divided into two main components: James's own, predominantly Irish, troops – a large number of English and Scots Jacobites served as officers, being augmented by a detachment of French officers who, in return for a local promotion, were tasked with helping to train the army – and a corps of several thousand French infantry which had been sent to Ireland by Louis XIV in return for the transfer of a similar number of Irishmen for French service, ostensibly to stiffen Jacobite backbones but in reality to ensure that the French crown maintained an influence on how the campaign was prosecuted. A Jacobite victory was desirable, but just not too soon, for the longer William could be distracted from Continental affairs the better it would suit France.

Although the campaign of 1689–90 had seen a general improvement in the condition of the Jacobite army, both as a result of experience gained in the field as well as the increase in *matériel* and military supplies received, in the main from France, it was still brittle with the quality of individual units varying greatly, thus making it potentially unreliable in combat.

The core of the army lay in two troops of Life Guards, each of 200 officers and men, and eight regiments of horse – heavy cavalry largely drawn from a 'squirearchy' formed by the landowning classes. The first three regiments: Tyrconnel's, Galmoy's and Sarsfield's each comprised nine troops of 53 men, for a regimental strength of 477 officers and other ranks; the remaining regiments each mustered six troops, for a regimental strength of 318. In addition, a troop of horse grenadiers was added to the Life Guards' establishment. Armed with a brace of pistols and a heavy broadsword, their relative inexperience was compensated by their natural ability in the saddle, being exhibited at Dromore and Cladyford as well as at the Boyne.

James's other mounted troops were formed into eight regiments of dragoons; equipped with lighter horses, they were used as mounted infantry, mainly for outpost duties or for holding terrain features. In the

Musketeer, King James's Regiment of Foot Guards. Commanded by William Dorrington, the Foot Guards were the core of Hamilton's Brigade. Unable to engage the Dutch Guards fully, they nevertheless resisted fiercely and gained time for Tyrconnel to deploy his cavalry against the Williamite centre. (Reconstruction copyright and courtesy of Robert Hall)

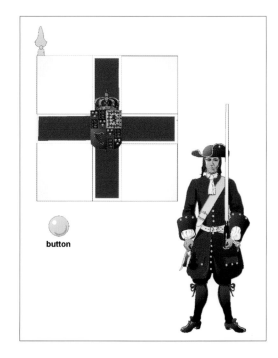

button

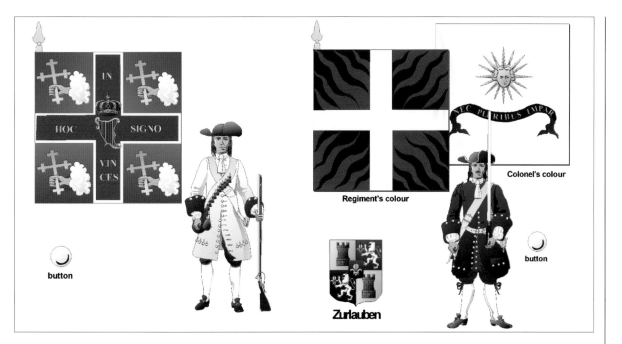

Regiment's colour

Colonel's colour

button

Zurlauben

button

absence of true cavalry, they would often be called upon to fight in a mounted role, but with mixed results. Again, like the horse regiments, the organization was unequal, with three regiments, Dongan's, O'Neill's and Luttrell's, forming eight troops of 60 men, for a regimental strength of 480 officers and other ranks, with the remaining five regiments each mustering six such troops.

The remainder of the army was organized into some 56 regiments of foot, nominally comprising a single battalion of 13 companies of 100 men each, organized on a ratio of three musketeers for each pikeman. Where possible, the 13th company was armed with flintlocks and equipped as grenadiers. There were, of course, some exceptions to this, for example the Irish Foot Guards and de Boisseleau's regiment of foot, both of which mustered two battalions.

A popular misconception is that the Jacobite army was exceptionally poorly equipped, that firearms were of bad quality and that to compensate for this shortcoming many of the army were forced to fight with 'half pikes' – improvised weapons made from scythe blades mounted on poles.

During the initial months of the war, the army did indeed suffer from bad organization and a lack of weapons. This state of affairs could only be alleviated by private purchase or the use of captured equipment. This situation was heavily underlined by the French commissary, Fumeron, in his early correspondence with Louvois, the French Minister of War. However, from May 1689, French convoys were beginning to deliver significant amounts of *matériel* and there was a tangible improvement in the equipment of the army. Again referring to the French archives, Fumeron, firstly in a letter dated 27 September 1689, states that of the main army, a total of 637 men were armed with 'half pikes': Edward Butler (120), Richard Butler (95), Lord Mountcashel (113), Richard Nugent (33), Lord Bellew (127), Dudley Bagenal (48), John Grace (18), Thomas Butler (75) and Lord Louth (8). Of the remaining 1,600 troops who had been issued with faulty muskets, almost half of these weapons were capable of repair,

Extract of the Review of the Royal Army, which took place on 1/2 October 1689. Sent by Commissary Fumeron with his letter dated 15 October 1689. Source: Archives Nationales, Depot de la Guerre, Ref A895, Document 1906(25)

Regiments of Foot	Captains	Lieutenants	Ensigns	NCOs	Drummers	Effectives	Serviceable Firearms	Pike/ Half Pike	Unarmed
Foot Guards (2 Bttns)	18	38	17	53	34	1,093	926	167	0
Antrim	10	13	9	21	10	513	411	46	56
Bagnal	10	10	10	26	12	460	256	204	0
Bellew	12	11	12	33	17	820	635	185	0
Boisseleau (2 Bttns)	37	32	25	52	26	952	676	276	0
Clancarty	11	12	11	25	11	220	202	18	0
Clanrickarde	12	12	12	26	13	681	436	201	44
Cormac O'Neill	26	26	27	53	24	1,205	710	290	205
Creagh	22	17	13	28	14	570	444	125	1
Dillon (2 Bttns)	29	23	20	43	34	1,236	641	380	215
Edward Butler	16	10	10	30	14	672	455	203	14
Eustace	19	19	12	35	15	733	395	208	130
Galway	6	12	11	26	9	418	297	91	30
Gormanston	8	14	10	26	6	521	404	105	12
Grace	16	14	9	26	7	439	267	163	9
Grand Prior	31	21	18	36	18	610	360	196	54
Hamilton	10	10	8	19	9	342	230	82	30
Kenmare	6	14	11	25	13	726	543	80	103
Kilmallock	16	16	14	30	15	651	438	213	0
Macarthy Mor	11	10	7	21	10	418	262	124	32
Mountcashel	9	7	8	24	7	331	195	136	0
Nugent	13	13	10	26	12	575	504	71	0
Oxburgh	10	9	6	20	10	286	205	80	1
Richard Butler	12	16	5	26	12	401	224	170	7
Slane	18	15	11	29	12	490	474	0	16
Thomas Butler	9	14	9	21	10	398	223	58	117
TOTAL	397	408	315	780	374	15,761	10,813	3,872	1,076

Regiments of Horse	Captains	Lieutenants	Cornets	Exempts	NCOs	Trumpeters	Effectives	Mounted and Armed	Dismounted/ Unarmed
Life Guards	0	2	2	4	16	4	161	161	0
Tyrconnell	11	8	9	0	9	6	365	365	0
Galmoy	12	16	8	0	9	7	315	303	12
Sarsfield	8	8	8	0	11	8	390	295	95
Parker	10	8	7	0	6	8	326	148	17
Abercorn	6	6	5	0	4	4	174	174	0
Luttrell	6	7	5	0	6	5	222	222	0
TOTAL	53	55	44	4	61	42	1,953	1,668	124

Regiments of Dragoons	Captains	Lieutenants	Cornets	NCOs	Drummers	Effectives	Mounted and Armed	Dismounted/ Unarmed
Dongan	9	10	9	28	12	406	388	18
Luttrell	5	1	2	14	8	233	215	18
Purcell	10	9	6	24	10	261	303	-42
Cotter	8	9	7	27	4	310	267	43
Clifford	9	13	4	20	9	303	113	190
TOTAL	41	42	28	113	43	1,513	1,286	227

whilst the remainder of the men were then issued with 'half pikes' from army stores.

By 15 October he was able to report that of the 15,761 infantrymen in the main Jacobite field army, some 10,813 were armed with serviceable firearms, whilst 3,872 were armed with either pikes or 'half pikes'. In the final analysis, as the Jacobite army went into winter quarters at the end of 1689, less than 10 per cent were inadequately armed.

To bolster James's position, six regiments of French infantry had been exchanged for a similar number of Irish troops (the embryonic Mountcashel Brigade): Famechon, Forez, La Marche, Mérode, Tournaisis and Zurlauben. The first named consisted of Walloons, with the next four comprising native French troops whilst the last was originally a Walloon

Plug bayonet, c.1680. Developed as a means of giving a musketeer protection against cavalry, the 'plug' bayonet fitted directly into the musket barrel, converting it into a polearm. Once used, however, it would require a period of relative calm for the musketeer to remove it and prepare his weapon for firing again. (Photograph courtesy of the Trustees, Royal Armouries, Leeds)

RIGHT Flintlock holster pistols, English, c.1685, by Robert Brooke. Each cavalry trooper carried a pair of such pistols in holsters mounted on his saddlebow. Their usage depended on how the trooper was trained; some styles favoured closing to contact with cold steel, others to pistol range, with one or both of the pistols being fired before entering combat. (Photograph courtesy of the Trustees, Royal Armouries, Leeds)

regiment, now predominantly manned by Germans and commanded by a Swiss. Although the overall usefulness of the French troops was compromised by instructions from Versailles, it was the actions of the Swiss Zurlauben that would allow the Jacobite army to escape capture at Duleek.

The final part of King James's army consisted of 18 artillery pieces, mainly 6lb guns, of which, according to most sources, 12 had been sent from the battlefield before the opening shots had been fired, whilst the remainder were attached to the French brigade. Outgunned and outclassed by the Williamite artillery train, James's artillery had no real effect on the battle.

THE WILLIAMITE FORCES

Despite the contentions of certain commentators, William's army was not part of a Protestant 'crusade'. With the exception of the Dutch, his major allies within the League of Augsburg were all Catholic states, and to have made such a declaration would have been tantamount to political suicide: the Alliance, and therefore all organized resistance to Louis XIV of France, would quite simply have collapsed.

For William, the most important part of his army was the contingent of troops supplied by the Dutch States General. Based around the three battalions of *Gardes te Voet,* the formation comprised five further foot battalions, nine cavalry regiments and a Guard Dragoon regiment. Well trained and equipped with modern weapons, the Dutch were a welcome reassurance against William's precarious position as King of England; in the two years of his reign, much had been promised to those who had engineered the 'Glorious Revolution' and little had been received: those who had turned their coats to oust King James could just as easily turn them once more to welcome him back. Dutch support, however, was not without its price, and in a move reminiscent of the agreement struck between Dublin and Versailles, several thousand English veterans were sent to Flanders under Marlborough.

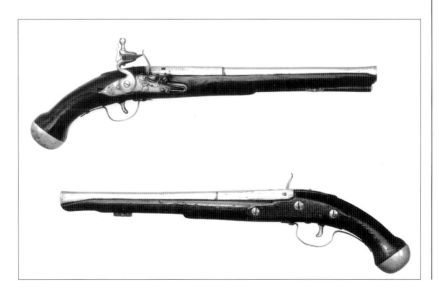

49

colonel's colour

major's colour

captain's colour

The cost of the Dutch troops was of no concern to William, for with Marlborough's arrival in the Low Countries, he had not only consolidated the Alliance's position there, but had just as importantly isolated the bulk of the English troops who might have had any cause to sympathize with his enemy. The deficit in troops for Ireland would need to be resolved by the raising of new regiments, and whilst they would be raw and in need of training, their loyalty would be to him. Following the relief of Derry, Schomberg's army was reinforced by these new battalions, and with minimal training their baptism of fire came not on the battlefield but rather in the camp at Dundalk, where an epidemic swept through their ranks.

Organized in a similar manner to their Jacobite counterparts, William's English troops comprised two troops of Life Guards, eight regiments of horse, two of dragoons and 16 regiments of foot. As has been stated, the majority of the English troops committed to Schomberg's army in late 1689 were newly raised units with minimal training. However, for the Boyne campaign William also brought over a cadre of several veteran regiments drawn both from the English establishment and from elements of the Anglo-Dutch Brigade, a formation of English troops that was maintained at the expense of the Dutch government.

The final component of William's 'English' army was a brigade of three regiments of foot which had been raised by the Earl of Meath, the Earl of Drogheda and Lord Lisburn.

In the period following the withdrawal of the Jacobite army to eastern Ulster, the defenders of Derry and Enniskillen were reorganized on a formal basis, with the former providing three regiments of foot (St John, Mitchelburne and Caulfield) whilst Enniskillen was able to muster a regiment of horse (Wolseley), two regiments of dragoons (Wynne and Cunningham) and again three regiments of foot (Gustavus Hamilton, Lloyd and Tiffin). Although disparaged by Schomberg as 'so many Croats', they would provide valuable service during the summer of 1690.

ABOVE, LEFT **Officer and grenadier, King William's Regiment of Dutch** *Gardes te Voet*. **The spearhead of the Williamite attack at the Boyne, the regiment had been issued new colours in 1688 which, to give them a more 'English' appearance, consisted of the Cross of St George on an orange field. As William was not yet king, the royal arms were replaced by the Order of the Garter. Trophies occupied the cantons to signify William's inevitable victory. (Reconstruction copyright and courtesy of Robert Hall)**

ABOVE, RIGHT **Musketeer, Sir John Hanmer's Regiment of English Foot. The leading regiment of Schomberg's second brigade, Hanmer's Regiment was caught in the fateful Jacobite cavalry charge that resulted in the Duke's death. (Reconstruction copyright and courtesy of Robert Hall)**

colonel's

other companies' colours

Officer and Musketeer, Brandenburg Regiment of Dutch Foot. Raised and commanded by William's cousin, Prince Albrecht of Brandenburg, this 'German' regiment formed part of Schomberg's second brigade with Hanmer's and Nassau's regiments. Advancing in echelon, it escaped attack as it crossed the Boyne. (Reconstruction copyright and courtesy of Robert Hall)

RIGHT Grenadier Corporal, Danish Foot Guards. As the spearhead of the Danish troops, the Guard Grenadiers came into combat early, beating off an attack by Jacobite Dragoons before consolidating their position and allowing other Danish units to cross the Boyne. (Reconstruction copyright and courtesy of Soren Henriksen)

FAR, RIGHT Musketeer, Danish *Fynske* Regiment of Foot. One of the Danish 'line' regiments, the anglicization of the unit's title became the foundation for the myth that a regiment of Finnish troops had fought for William at the Boyne. (Reconstruction copyright and courtesy of Soren Henriksen)

For his invasion of England in 1688, William had recruited heavily amongst Huguenot refugees who had fled France following the revocation of the Edict of Nantes, comprising a regiment of horse (Duke of Schomberg) and three of foot (Cambon, Caillemotte, Melonière). It was felt that the Frenchmen would be amongst the more reliable of William's forces and indeed, it was their furious mêlée against the Irish horse that would prove to be one of the turning points of the battle.

The next major component of William's army was a force of about 7,000 Danish mercenaries. Although his kingdom was geographically small, King Christian V of Denmark maintained a relatively large standing army and was willing to supplement his revenues by hiring out his troops to foreign powers. The problem that William faced was that at the time he needed to hire the troops, Denmark was on the brink of a war with Sweden over their respective interests in Holstein in northern Germany. The crucial point was that his Dutch and Imperialist allies supported the Swedes whilst Denmark was allied to France. With indifferent support from Versailles, the Danes were forced to back down. Consequently Christian began to look for suitable employers for a large proportion of his army, and on 30 September 1689 a treaty was ratified between London and Copenhagen. Originally comprising three regiments of horse and nine of foot, because of the capture of several transports en

route to England, the Queen's and Oldenburg regiments were merged, and a total of eight foot regiments saw service in Ireland.

Finally, the army included an artillery train of some 36 guns, all of which were of heavier calibre than those used by the Jacobites. With James withdrawing the bulk of his cannon before the battle, the Williamite gunners deployed on the rising ground to the north of the Boyne would enjoy total superiority during the initial bombardment of the Jacobite positions.

William's army was an amalgam of differing equipment and tactical doctrines. The Dutch and Danes were well trained and predominantly armed with flintlocks, the English and Ulster troops with matchlocks and pikes; the Ulstermen were fighting for their religion and way of life, the Danes for money. William was not an exceptional general, but his charisma bound the army together in a way that superseded his command ability.

It must be noted that the two armies were not divided along strictly religious lines. To cite two examples, Sir Michael Creagh, the Protestant Lord Mayor of Dublin, raised a regiment of foot for the Jacobite service whilst the Earl of Meath, likewise a Protestant, also originally commissioned his regiment to serve James, but on being turned down by Tyrconnel for political reasons, then offered his men to William, whom they served with singular distinction.

A note on uniforms

With the exception of the foreign contingents, the bulk of the protagonists on both sides fought in the traditional red of the English army, differing only in the choice of a field-sign worn in the brim of their hats. To symbolize their alliance with France, the Jacobites wore a white cockade of cloth or paper whilst the Williamites, as was their practice in Flanders, wore a sprig of green.

Also, given their reliance on French supplies, where the Jacobites were unable to obtain the desired red coats, they wore uniforms of *gris-mesle*, a cloth issued to the French army which, flecked with blue threads, varied in shade from white to pale grey, often being described as both.

Partizan, French, *c.*1680, with sun motif decoration. Carried as a sign of rank as well as a weapon and means of forming troops, this example carries the motif of the 'Sun in Splendour' – the personal emblem of Louis XIV of France, the Sun King. (Photograph courtesy of the Trustees, Royal Armouries, Leeds)

ORDERS OF BATTLE

JACOBITE ORDER OF BATTLE

TAKEN FROM COOKSTOWN REVIEW, 24 JUNE 1690

His Majesty, James II, King of England, Scotland and Ireland.

IRISH FORCES

Regiments of Horse:
Life Guards
Duke of Tyrconnel's
Viscount Galmoy's
Colonel Sutherland's
Colonel Parker's
Colonel Sarsfield's
Earl of Abercorn's

Regiments of Dragoons:
Brigadier Maxwell's
Sir Niall O'Neill's
Lord Dongan's
Lord Clare's
Colonel Clifford's
Colonel Carroll's

Regiments of Foot:
Foot Guards (Right)
Earl of Antrim's (Right)
Lord Bellew's
Gordon O'Neill's
Lord Louth's
Lord Grand-Prior's
John Grace's
Art McMahon's
Hugh McMahon's
John Hamilton's
Earl of Westmeath's
Sir Michael Creagh's
Roger MacElligott's
Charles O'Brien's
Maj. Gen. Boisseleau's
Dudley Bagenal's
Earl of Tyrone's
Lord Slane's
Henry Dillon's
Earl of Clanrickarde's
Lord Galway's
Walter Bourke's
Lord Gormanston's
Richard Nugent's

FRENCH FORCES
Regiments of Foot:
Famechon – 1,055
Forez – 1,097
La Marche – 1,097
Mérode – 855
Tournaisis – 1,097
Zurlauben – 2,090

WILLIAMITE ORDER OF BATTLE

TAKEN FROM FINGLAS REVIEW, 5 JULY 1690

His Majesty, William III, King of England, Scotland and Ireland.

ANGLO-IRISH FORCES:

Regiments of Horse:
Life Guards – 368
Count Schomberg's – 242
Earl of Oxford's – 368
Sir John Lanier's – 360
Colonel Byerley's – 244
Colonel Coy's – 236
Colonel Langston's – 225
Colonel Russell's – 242
Colonel Villiers' – 245
Colonel Wolseley's – 423
Captain Harbord's Troop – 38

Regiments of Dragoons:
Sir Albert Cunningham's – 358
Colonel Leveson's – 246
Colonel Matthews' – 406
Colonel Wynne's – 260

Regiments of Foot:
Lieutenant General Douglas' – 648
Major General Kirke's – 666
Brigadier Stuart's – 660
Brigadier Trelawney's – 553
Earl of Drogheda's – 660
Earl of Meath's – 678
Lord George Hamilton's – 583
Lord Lisburn's – 611
Sir Henry Bellasis' – 628
Sir John Hanmer's – 593
Colonel Beaumont's – 526
Colonel Brewer's – 571
Colonel Deering's – 600
Colonel Erle's – 693
Colonel Foulkes' – 439
Colonel Hamilton's – 560
Colonel Hastings' – 606
Colonel Herbert's – 600
Colonel Lloyd's – 652
Colonel Mitchelburne's – 664
Colonel St John's – 589
Colonel Tiffin's – 625

DUTCH FORCES
Regiments of Horse:
Gardes te Paard – 145
Lord Portland's – 357
Monopvillan's – 171
Lt. Gen. Ginkel's – 152
Scholk's – 167
Van Oyen's – 164
Reideffel's – 174
Rancour's – 178
Nyenburg's – 175

Regiments of Dragoons:
Eppinger's – 621

Regiments of Foot:
Gardes te Voet (inc cadets) – 1,931
Van Graben's – 490
Brandenburg – 631
Nassau–Saarbrücken–Ottweiler – 652
Colonel Babington's – 416
Colonel Cutts' – 543

DANISH FORCES:
Regiments of Horse:
Donop's – 263
Juel's – 268
Sehested's – 281

Regiments of Foot:
Garden til Fods – 698
Dronningen (Queen's) – 634*
Prince Frederick's – 555
Prince Christian's – 547
Prince Georg's – 547
Zealand – 527
Jutland – 554
Fünen – 519
(*) Later merged with the Oldenburg Regiment.

HUGUENOT FORCES:
Regiments of Horse:
Duke of Schomberg's – 395

Regiments of Foot:
Colonel Cambon's – 640
Colonel Caillemotte's – 562
Brigadier Melonière's – 529

OPPOSING PLANS

THE JACOBITE PLAN

Following the withdrawal from the Moyry Pass, and possibly drawing upon recollections of the indecision that had plagued him, with such dire consequences in 1688, James was determined to at least make a demonstration against the Williamites, rather than to simply follow the advice of his advisors whose suggestion was for the army to retire across the Shannon and let William's forces exhaust themselves in protracted siege and guerrilla warfare. As long as he had 'an army in being' James could delay as long as he chose, whilst William, with his throne insecure and as head of a military coalition, simply could not afford to spend a significant amount of time in Ireland. With Flanders as the main theatre of operations against France, he could not afford to linger in Ireland – every day that passed was crucial.

A Cavalry Skirmish by Jan Wyck. This painting shows the confused nature of a mêlée – the troopers are literally touching each other with their pistol barrels before opening fire. (Collection Ulster Museum Belfast, courtesy Trustees NMGNI)

Backsword with 'orb' mark, European, dated 1689. The standard cavalry weapon of both armies, this example features a wire-wrapped hilt, a two-piece hand guard and an orb-shaped pommel. It was most likely the weapon of an ordinary trooper. (Photograph courtesy of the Trustees, Royal Armouries, Leeds)

Given the disparity in numbers between the two armies, James knew that his only realistic option was to engage the enemy in close terrain, which could be used to somewhat nullify William's numerical advantage, and, north of Dublin, only one such position remained to him – the Boyne Valley.

Whilst his confidence held, James proposed to fight a defensive battle, and accordingly pitched his camp on the Hill of Donore, overlooking the southern bank of the Boyne. In order to channel the Williamite forces, the town of Drogheda and the hamlet of Oldbridge were occupied and prepared for defence, and, based on an inaccurate assumption that the river upstream from Oldbridge was unfordable, troops were sent to destroy the bridge at Slane and thereby deny that crossing point to the enemy. Preparations were then made for the army to deploy forward, so that any enemy forces that managed to cross the river could be immediately counter-attacked and defeated before they could be reinforced. In terms of manpower, James had the inferior force but, spearheaded by his veteran French troops, he felt that he could gain local superiority where needed and hold the fords.

At the council of war, the lack of adequate Jacobite reconnaissance soon came to light, when it was found that the Boyne was in fact passable above Oldbridge – there was a ford a few miles to the south-west at Rossnaree. Reactions were mixed. James felt that a small mounted piquet should be sent there to keep the ford under observation, whilst Léry de Girardin, the French officer in command of the army's left wing, felt that a significant force of cavalry should be detached to defend the crossing. Eventually, having persuaded James that there was a real threat, Léry de Girardin sent Sir Niall O'Neill's dragoon regiment to guard the ford. This lack of local information would cause problems during the battle and is inexcusable, not only because of the grace period in which the Jacobites had had to prepare their positions, but also because Lords Bellew, Louth and Slane, three of James's regimental

Mellifont Abbey. Hidden from the view of the Jacobite army, this former Cistercian monastery was used as William's headquarters before the battle. (Office of Public Works)

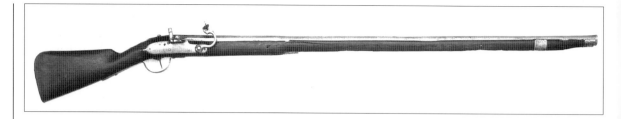

commanders, were all prominent local landowners, and it would have been assumed that they had a knowledge of the area.

In summary, James had occupied as advantageous a position as was possible, given the information available to him. The main crossing points had been garrisoned and fortified whilst the main body of the army was deployed well enough forward to permit an immediate counter-attack on any Williamite bridgeheads before they could be developed, and yet was far enough to the rear to fall outside the effective range of the Williamite artillery.

THE WILLIAMITE PLAN

At William's headquarters at Mellifont Abbey there was an air of tension, not simply as a result of the impending battle but also because of the strained relationships between William's Dutch and English commanders, which continued to fester as a result of his predilection for favouring his Dutch advisors over his English or Scots ones.

The council was inevitably divided. On the one hand the Duke of Schomberg, supported by the majority of the English officers present, counselled a limited, holding attack between Oldbridge and Drogheda, whilst the bulk of the army manoeuvred against the Jacobite left flank by way of Slane, eventually coming in behind the enemy army and cutting off its line of retreat. On the other, Count Solms, commander of the Dutch *Gardes te Voet*, contemptuous of the Franco-Irish forces, advocated a direct all-out assault, intended to rupture the Jacobite lines and force a passage straight through them irrespective of casualties.

William, however, had his own plan: earlier that evening a Jacobite deserter had been interrogated and questioned as to the size of the Jacobite army – 50,000 men was the reply. William then asked the Irishman what he estimated the strength of his own army to be, and based upon the answer to this question, he was able to deduce the size of the opposing army.

By now aware of his own numerical superiority, William decided upon a three-pronged attack whereby Meinhard, Count Schomberg (second son of the Duke), was detailed to take the right-wing cavalry and Brigadier Charles Trelawney's brigade of foot (a total of about 7,000 men) and effect a crossing of the Boyne in the area of Slane. The Duke of Schomberg, commanding the centre (about 20,000 men),

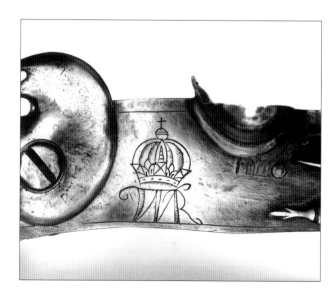

would soften up the Jacobite positions with a concentrated and over-whelming artillery bombardment and, with his troops' advance concealed by a ravine (later to be known as King William's Glen), then launch a series of attacks across the river, between Oldbridge and Yellow Island. William meanwhile, at the head of the left wing (approximately 8,000 men), would follow another channel at Drybridge and then cross the Boyne below Yellow Island, thereby turning the Jacobite right flank.

Crucial to the plan was that all components should complete their manoeuvres and arrive in position at the same time, roughly 9.00am, when, because of the low tide, all known river crossings would be practicable. He therefore dismissed Schomberg's subsequent suggestion that his son's force should set off at midnight, which would have placed Count Schomberg in position to attack the Jacobite flank, long before the other forces had deployed.

Even at this late stage, on the eve of battle, William could not bring himself to confide his full plans to his English officers but was fully aware that not to do so, whilst explaining himself fully to his other commanders, would be committing a grave error – both militarily and for the morale of the army. On calling the council of war to an end, he told those present that they would receive their complete orders in written form later that evening, and that this restriction would be placed on all officers including Schomberg who was still second in command of the army. Needless to say this did not sit well with the old soldier, who was heard to remark that 'this was the first that had ever been sent him', in other words that he was used to sharing the confidence of both his superiors and his subordinates.

William's plan was neither the endorsement nor the rebuttal of Schomberg's plan, but rather a reflection of his penchant for complicated battlefield manoeuvres. It was ambitious, and, like the Jacobite plan, did not take into account the local terrain, which could easily have had – and almost did have – catastrophic effects on the outcome of the battle.

THE BATTLE

THE FLANK MARCH

At a little before 5.00am on the morning of 1 July, as the sounds of reveille rang out around Mellifont and Tullyallen, and the majority of William's troops began to stir, a force of a little under 7,000 men under Meinhard, Count Schomberg, who had awoken three hours earlier, set off on their march around the Jacobite left flank.

There have been many interpretations of William's intentions for this flank march – that it was a simple feint, designed to draw off the enemy strength from the main engagement, that it was a manoeuvre intended to cross into the Jacobite rear and thereby cut their line of retreat, or that it was part of a preconceived pincer movement aimed at shattering King James's army by delivering a series of coordinated attacks.

Once the composition of Count Schomberg's force is examined in detail, it becomes readily apparent that the first explanation is unlikely, and that the reality is a combination of the remaining two possibilities. Under his command, Schomberg had nine regiments of Dutch cavalry totalling some 1,600 men, including the *Gardes te Paard* and *Gardes Dragonders* regiments as well as seven regiments of English cavalry, comprising a further 2,100 men, which included the Life Guards, the Earl of Oxford's 'Blue' Regiment and his own regiment of horse. To these mounted troops were added the five English foot battalions of Trelawney's brigade (Kirke's, Trelawney's, Erle's, Hastings' and Herbert's), which increased the force by a further 3,100 men, to which was attached a small train of light artillery for support. The column was therefore primarily intended as an aggressive

The heights above Rossnaree, O'Neill's first position. From the heights, O'Neill had an unparalleled view of the area and was able to observe Count Schomberg's approach, before moving downhill to dispute the crossing. (Author's photograph)

THE BATTLE OF THE BOYNE: 1 JULY 1690

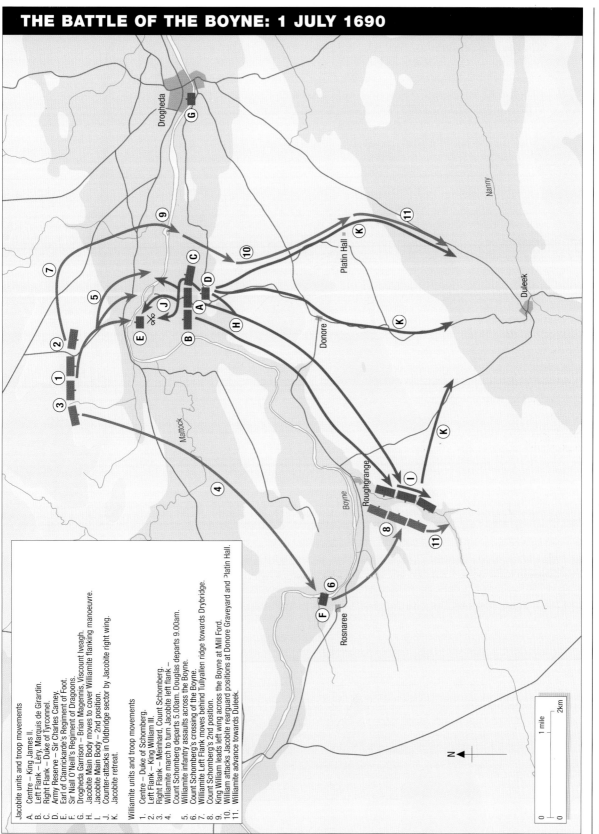

Jacobite units and troop movements

A. Centre – King James II.
B. Left Flank – Léry, Marquis de Girardin.
C. Right Flank – Duke of Tyrconnel.
D. Army Reserve – Sir Charles Carney.
E. Earl of Clanrickarde's Regiment of Foot.
F. Sir Niall O'Neill's Regiment of Dragoons.
G. Drogheda Garrison – Brian Magennis, Viscount Iveagh.
H. Jacobite Main Body moves to cover Williamite flanking manoeuvre.
I. Jacobite Main Body – 2nd position.
J. Counter-attacks in Oldbridge sector by Jacobite right wing.
K. Jacobite retreat.

Williamite units and troop movements

1. Centre – Duke of Schomberg.
2. Left Flank – King William III.
3. Right Flank – Meinhard, Count Schomberg.
4. Williamite march to turn Jacobite left flank –
   Count Schomberg departs 5.00am. Douglas departs 9.00am.
5. Williamite infantry assaults across the Boyne.
6. Count Schomberg's crossing of the Boyne.
7. Williamite Left Flank moves behind Tullyallen ridge towards Drybridge.
8. Count Schomberg's 2nd position.
9. King William leads left wing across the Boyne at Mill Ford.
10. William attacks Jacobite rearguard positions at Donore Graveyard and Platin Hall.
11. Williamite advance towards Duleek.

59

cavalry force which, as has been illustrated, contained some of William's best cavalry units, and was therefore eminently suited for the interdiction of the Jacobite line of retreat but which could also, should circumstances dictate, easily convert to a more aggressive role.

Of these two possibilities, and given William's distrust of his English officers – and by definition their troops – the fact that over three-quarters of Count Schomberg's men were English would suggest that William intended the force to play an important rather than a pivotal role in the battle and would seem to indicate that Schomberg's instructions, at least initially, were to cross the Boyne and interdict the Jacobite army's line of retreat.

The column moved off slowly into the early morning mist, preceded, presumably, by scouts taken from Captain Pownel's troop of Leveson's dragoons who had conducted the previous day's reconnaissance towards Slane.

Moving south-westwards, the troops were slowed by the uneven terrain and the obvious need to travel at the same speed as the artillery train. Crossing the Mattock, a tributary of the Boyne, Schomberg paused at the small village of Monknewton and sent out scouting parties west towards Slane and the Boyne along his intended line of march. A cautious officer like his father, Schomberg was taking nothing for granted, making sure that the area was clear of enemy troops as well as searching for alternative crossing points over the Boyne following the destruction of the bridge at Slane.

The Williamite column continued its progress towards the river bend, marching across the *Brugh na Bóinne* – the Palace of the Boyne – a collection of prehistoric burial mounds centred around the tumuli of Newgrange, Dowth and Knowth. At around 8.00am, having out-distanced his infantry and artillery support, and having taken some three hours to cover a mere four miles, Schomberg's advance guard came into sight of a cluster of watermills that marked the crossing at Rossnaree.

As the Anglo-Dutch column came into sight of the ford, they were observed by the officers and men of Sir Niall O'Neill's dragoon regiment waiting on the heights above Rossnaree, from where the Jacobite horsemen enjoyed a panoramic view of the northern bank and the approaches to the ford.

O'Neill's dragoons, raised in 1687 and numbering around 480 effectives, was regarded as among the best of the Jacobite regiments, having fought in Sarsfield's campaign to recapture Sligo the previous year. The 32-year-old regimental colonel, Sir Niall O'Neill, was himself a colourful character – an amalgam of 17th-century nobleman and Gaelic warlord.

Perhaps the idea of defending a river crossing appealed to O'Neill's 'Gaelic side' as, after despatching a courier to King James's headquarters with the news of the attack at Rossnaree, he led his men down from the heights towards the ford.

On the other side of the river, according to Story in his *Impartial History of the Affairs of Ireland*, 'As some of our Horse marched to the River, there stood a regiment of the Enemies Dragoons (sent thither overnight) nigh the bank on the other side who fired upon us and then thought to have retreated to their main Body but before they could do that, they were flanked in a Lane, and about seventy of them cut off.'

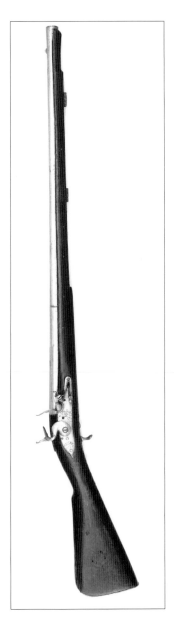

Flintlock military musket, English, c.1685–89, James II cavalry carbine. Weapons of similar design to this flintlock carbine by Bankes were the standard firearm for the majority of mounted units at the Boyne. (Photograph courtesy of the Trustees, Royal Armouries, Leeds)

Schomberg's aide, St Felix, who was to carry news of the successful crossing to William, was more detailed when he wrote that the Count,

> detached a hundred horse grenadiers to march to the ford in formation to draw enemy fire. At the same time he advanced with the Royal dragoon regiment … They were no sooner at the ford then the enemy opened fire on them. The Count, from the riverbank, urged them to cross now. The enemy, some 1,200 horsemen, came again 'à la charge' but the Count noticed that the enemy fire grew ragged after this firing and called out to the dragoons that they must take the ford by force; at the same time he plunged into the river, sword in hand, at the head of the dragoons. He charged the enemy so well and with such spirit that he pushed them back on each other and pursued them for 2 miles towards where the enemy was drawn up in battle formations.

The crossing was neither as simple nor as straightforward as these commentators portray it to have been. As they descended towards the plain, O'Neill's men dismounted and began to approach the ford on foot, whilst, on the other side of the crossing and with no supporting infantry present, Count Schomberg ordered the *Gardes Dragonders* – William's Dutch Guard Dragoons, and the strongest regiment under his command – to force the passage and sweep the Jacobites aside.

Initially, Abraham van Eppinger, in command of the Dutchmen, elected to simply storm across the ford and, using converged horse grenadiers from each of his regiment's companies, he threw his men eagerly into the assault. Plunging into the river from the high northern bank, which had prohibited a mounted attack, the Dutchmen were soon disordered and came under a heavy fire from the Irish dragoons.

Unable to make any headway, and despite their superiority in numbers, the Williamite troops withdrew and a desultory skirmish ensued, with O'Neill gaining precious time with each minute that passed.

Some time after 9.00am, as the sound of cannon fire began to echo over the hills around Oldbridge, Count Schomberg's own guns finally came up and were quickly deployed for action. With artillery fire falling amongst the Jacobite dragoons, tragedy soon struck: O'Neill fell, his thigh shattered by Williamite roundshot. With their leader rendered *hors de combat* and carried dying from the field, the dragoons' resistance began to slacken and they too soon mounted up and quit the field, conceding the crossing to Schomberg's forces, having successfully held the enemy at bay for a little over an hour.

O'Neill's mortal wound – he died a week later in Waterford – shows the brittle nature of James's 'Gaelic Irish' troops. Their loyalty was not to a king or a commander appointed by him but to their clan chief. In this respect they were similar to the Scottish Highlanders with whom they shared a language and culture. While their leaders ordered them to fight they would, but with their loss and despite the regimental organization to which they submitted, there was no real structure available which would facilitate an immediate change in command.

As O'Neill's dragoons began to fall back towards Donore, Schomberg began to push his troops across the river and consolidate his position and, as his men began to form up on the southern bank of the Boyne, he sent his aide St Felix with a message to William with an account of the

Rossnaree, looking towards Count Schomberg's probable crossing point. After he had passed the rolling countryside around Newgrange, Count Schomberg was faced both with a steep descent to the Boyne before he could ford the river, and a Jacobite blocking force holding the southern bank. (Author's photograph)

Rossnaree, the northern bank of the Boyne. This high northern bank prevented Count Schomberg from 'rushing' O'Neill's troops with cavalry, and forced him to rely on dismounted dragoons to clear the way. (Author's photograph)

engagement and the news that the ford at Rossnaree had been secured. Although he had succeeded in his initial instructions Count Schomberg had, by allowing his force to straggle and thereby attacking whilst his force was strung out on the line of march, also compromised them, for the Jacobite high command was now aware of the attempt to turn their army's left flank.

WILLIAM'S HEADQUARTERS

As the right wing of the army marched off into the early morning mist, the main body of the army came to life, preparing for the conflict to come. In all probability, there was a second gathering of William's senior officers, in which he clarified his plans for the assault across the Boyne. Supported by a major artillery bombardment, the Dutch *Gardes te Voet*, under William's cousin Heinrich, Count Solms-Braunfels, and massing almost 2,000 men, would advance towards the river along a defile which would soon be known as 'King William's Glen' and, crossing at low tide,

would attack the Jacobite positions around the village of Oldbridge. Under this cover they would be able to approach the river more or less unseen by the enemy and therefore deny them time in which to react to the assault.

A second column, consisting of some 1,500 cavalry under the command of Godard, Baron Ginkel, would, in a similar move, approach the river via another defile at Drybridge. In a coordinated attack with the Dutch Guards, and hopefully with a similar element of surprise, Ginkel would pin the enemy line in position whilst the main body of the army, a composite force of English, Dutch, Irish and Huguenot troops under the command of the Duke of Schomberg, and a brigade of about 6,000 Danes under the command of the Duke of Württemberg-Neustadt, would strike at the enemy centre, by this time denuded of troops which had been diverted to meet the flanking forces, and shatter it. William himself would remain in command of the army reserve, a force numbering around 8,000 effectives.

THE HILL OF DONORE

Some time after, James's own council of war broke up and, plagued by indecision, he called a second council of war during which he decided to withdraw from the field and pull back towards Dublin via Duleek, a small village where several roads converged, before crossing the river Nanny by the Magdalene Bridge. It was a dangerous bottleneck that would have a crucial impact on the later movements of the Jacobite army.

Accordingly, orders were given for the baggage train to begin its move southwards by the most direct route. However, based upon an incorrect assumption regarding the location of William's main body, it was agreed that the army, beginning with the left wing under the Marquis Léry de Girardin – comprising the French brigade as well as three mounted Irish regiments (Viscount Galmoy's and Patrick Sarsfield's regiments of horse and Maxwell's dragoons) – would march west towards Slane and then fall back to the south. As this manoeuvre took place, the main body of troops would move to their left, thereby **63**

The Battle of the Boyne (VS2838). With the Jacobite infantry massing on the southern bank, and the Williamites advancing through the river, this scene may depict the battle from Grove Island, with the Huguenots advancing on the left flank of the *Gardes te Voet*, already attacking Oldbridge. (With kind permission of the Trustees, Atlas Van Stolk, Rotterdam)

continuing to cover the ford at Oldbridge, whilst occupying the ground vacated by the marching troops. No direct mention seems to have been made regarding the men garrisoning Drogheda and Oldbridge, but it is reasonable to assume that they would have been withdrawn as part of the redeployment of Tyrconnel's wing.

There was chaos in the Jacobite ranks, and it wasn't until a little after 8.00am, when the troops began to strike camp and then possibly half an hour later, that the message came which would turn the Franco-Irish plans on their head. As the reality of the Williamite attack at Rossnaree began to dawn upon James and his advisors, their anxiety about a threat to the army's rear and line of retreat became real rather than implied, and so, instead of preparing to withdraw, de Lauzun immediately led several thousand of the army's best troops to block Count Schomberg's progress.

To reinforce de Lauzun, James immediately instructed the French officer Laisné, who was in command of the Jacobite artillery, to detach a battery in support of the left wing. Laisné in turn (according to a letter written a week after the battle to Louvois, the French Minister of War) sent the commissary Montgrizy with six cannon – four 'Irish' pieces and two 'French' – to assist de Lauzun. In an echo of Louvois's own instructions, Laisné then states that he ordered Montgrizy to take the utmost care of the 'French' guns – what his instructions were with reference to the 'Irish' guns are not recorded.

Across the valley, observers amongst the Williamite forces saw the movement of a significant number of men westwards which – even if they had been able to tell their nationality – could have meant only one thing: that they were marching to engage the flanking force at Rossnaree.

William was placed in a quandary: whatever his original plans may have been for Meinhard Schomberg's column, it was now in danger of being overwhelmed by the enemy and needed to be urgently reinforced. Accordingly, and by way of support, he sent Lieutenant General James Douglas, at the head of five English battalions towards the ford at Rossnaree – even at this stage, William would not compromise or alter his position over the reliability of his English troops. Schomberg was in a difficult but not impossible situation. And therefore there was no reason to alter the main plan of attack – with almost 11,000 men, Count Schomberg would command almost a third of the army.

Back on Donore, James and his staff watched this movement of enemy troops with dread. Perhaps with thoughts of the recent French victory of Fleurus in mind – ten days previously, Marshal Luxembourg had scored a crushing victory over the Dutch general Waldeck when, dividing his forces in the face of the enemy, he left a weakened centre and, marching his main body of troops under concealment, redeployed them on Waldeck's flanks, and then in an overwhelming attack, routed the enemy, causing almost 20,000 casualties at a cost of only 3,000 Frenchmen – James issued a momentous order: believing that Douglas's troops constituted the beginning of a movement by the whole Williamite army, he ordered the main body of his own army including the reserve under Sir Charles Carney to follow de Lauzun towards Rossnaree. What must be stressed is that this was not James seeking to avoid combat, far from it; his intention was to engage the Williamites as they crossed the Boyne and defeat them in detail.

As his troops marched along Redmountain, de Lauzun had a perfect view down towards Rossnaree, and, as he later wrote to the Marquis de Seignelay, the French Minister of Marine:

> *From here I saw that the dragoons that I had left at the bridge of Slane had been pushed back and that the enemy had already crossed the ford this side of Slane and that they were passing in columns, cavalry, infantry, cannon, either making for Dublin or for our rear. The King came there and ordered us to adopt a battle line to our left and to make space on my right, leading to the river. Then I could either shadow the march of the enemy towards Dublin or attack them as soon as Milord Tyrconnel, who commanded the left wing, arrived.*

What would have been apparent to an interested observer was that the battle had now become a race between both armies as to who could strike a telling blow against an isolated enemy force. It reaffirms the fact that on a day where a good level of information was crucial, the Jacobites believed that they were neither withdrawing nor refusing to give battle but rather that, as far as they were aware, they were marching to meet and engage the main enemy body.

James's decision would prove to be one of the crucial events of the day. An adequate pre-battle reconnaissance would have shown that the 'open left flank' which the Jacobites had believed to exist was actually exceptionally close and rough terrain, perfect for defence, where the quality of ground would offset the attacker's numerical superiority. Had this been the case, James might have changed his mind again, and left the main body facing Oldbridge. The presence of twice the number of Jacobite troops – especially cavalry – would have had a significant effect on how the battle developed around Oldbridge.

Orders were then sent to Tyrconnel, advising him of the King's decision and ordering him to observe the enemy on the northern bank across from Oldbridge before himself withdrawing in the wake of the main body of the army.

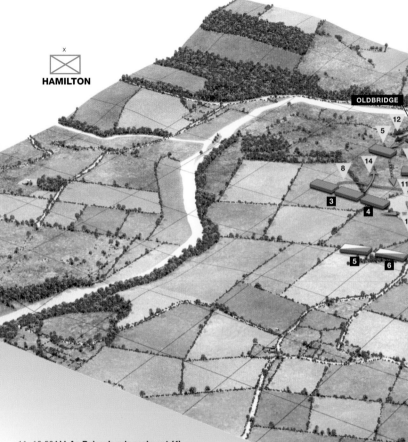

WILLIAMITES

A *Gardes te Voet* (Dutch – three battalions and attached cadets)

B De la Melonière's Regiment of Foot (Huguenot – one battalion)

C Caillemotte's Regiment of Foot (Huguenot – one battalion)

D Cambon's Regiment of Foot (Huguenot – one battalion)

E Sir John Hanmer's Regiment of Foot (English – one battalion)

F Nassau-Saarbrücken-Ottweiler Regiment of Foot (Dutch – one battalion)

G Brandenburg Regiment of Foot (Dutch – one battalion)

H Artillery Train

I Colonel John Mitchelbourne's Regiment of Foot (Londonderry – one battalion)

J Colonel Thomas St.John's Regiment of Foot (Londonderry – one battalion)

K Lord George Hamilton's Regiment of Foot (Enniskillen – one battalion)

L Colonel Zachariah Tiffin's Regiment of Foot (Enniskillen – one battalion)

M Danish Brigade (eight foot battalions, three horse regiments)

N Williamite left wing (three regiments of horse, three regiments of dragoons, 10 battalions of foot)

O Lt. Gen. Ginkel's Brigade (six cavalry regiments)

HAMILTON

OLDBRIDGE

TYRCONNEL

BERWICK

SHELDON

▼ EVENTS

1. 8.00AM **Williamite left wing (N) moves towards Drybridge, under cover of early morning mist. Ginkel's cavalry brigade is unable to cross at Mill Ford due to the condition of the crossing.**

2. 9.00AM **Williamite artillery train (H) commences preparatory bombardment of Jacobite positions at Oldbridge.**

3. 10.00AM **Williamite artillery ceases fire. Dutch *Gardes te Voet* (A) debouch from King William's Glen and advance to the river opposite Oldbridge.**

4. 10.10AM **Led by grenadier companies, Dutch Guards (A) cross the river under fire from Clanrickarde's Jacobite foot (2) defending Oldbridge.**

5. 10.25AM **Pressed by the Dutch Guards (A), Clanrickarde's (2) troops begin to slowly withdraw from Oldbridge, continually halting to reform and fire at the Williamite troops.**

6. 10.30AM **Dorrington leads King James's Foot Guards (1) forward in support of Clanrickarde (2).**

7. 10.30AM **Huguenot Brigade (B–C–D) begins to cross the Boyne at Grove Island.**

8. 10.30AM **Hamilton orders the remainder of the Jacobite foot forward preparatory to a counter-attack against the Dutch *Gardes te Voet* (A).**

9. 10.40AM **Leading elements of both Guards regiments close in hand-to-hand combat.**

10. 10.45AM **Anglo-Dutch Brigade (E–F–G) prepares to cross the Boyne east of Grove Island.**

11. 10.50AM **As Boisseleau's regiment (4) advances; both the Guards (1) and Clanrickarde (2) continue to fall back.**

12. 10.50AM **Dutch *Gardes te Voet* begin to consolidate their position around Oldbridge.**

13. 10.50AM **Hamilton leads Antrim's regiment of foot to engage the Williamite units in the process of crossing the Boyne. They begin an ineffective fire at long range.**

14. 11.00AM **Boisseleau (4) is unable to bring his troops into action alongside the Guards (1) and Clanrickarde (2), who are engaged with the *Gardes te Voet* (A) and de la Melonière's Huguenot foot (B).**

15. 11.15AM **The Jacobite front line (1–2–4) buckles under the pressure of the enemy firepower and starts to withdraw.**

16. 11.15AM **The Londonderry/Enniskillen regiments (I–J–K–L) move westwards from their position in the Williamite second line, so as to bring them opposite Oldbridge in order to cross the Boyne behind the *Gardes te Voet* (A).**

17. 11.15AM **The Danish Brigade moves forward to its crossing point opposite Yellow Island.**

18. 11.20AM **Antrim's Regiment (3) seeing its supports withdraw, and in view of the developing threat from the Danish Brigade, pulls back from the river line.**

THE WILLIAMITE ATTACK

1 July 1690, viewed looking north to south (and vice-versa), showing the Williamite crossings of the Boyne at Oldbridge and Grove Island, and the initial Jacobite responses.

Note: Gridlines are shown at intervals of 250m

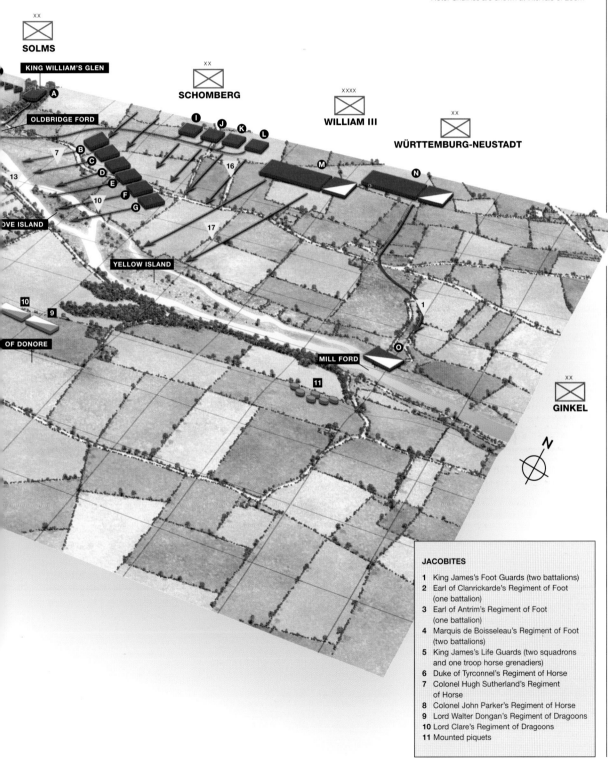

SOLMS

KING WILLIAM'S GLEN

OLDBRIDGE FORD

SCHOMBERG

WILLIAM III

WÜRTTEMBURG-NEUSTADT

OVE ISLAND

YELLOW ISLAND

OF DONORE

MILL FORD

GINKEL

N

JACOBITES

1 King James's Foot Guards (two battalions)
2 Earl of Clanrickarde's Regiment of Foot (one battalion)
3 Earl of Antrim's Regiment of Foot (one battalion)
4 Marquis de Boisseleau's Regiment of Foot (two battalions)
5 King James's Life Guards (two squadrons and one troop horse grenadiers)
6 Duke of Tyrconnel's Regiment of Horse
7 Colonel Hugh Sutherland's Regiment of Horse
8 Colonel John Parker's Regiment of Horse
9 Lord Walter Dongan's Regiment of Dragoons
10 Lord Clare's Regiment of Dragoons
11 Mounted piquets

In a scant few hours, the situation at Oldbridge had been transformed. With a little under 7,000 men, Tyrconnel was charged to hold an area of ground previously defended by almost four times that number! As his troops filed into their new positions, and as he looked out across the valley, where the early morning mist was beginning to dissipate, the Duke undoubtedly felt a growing sense of unease.

THE WILLIAMITES MOVE

With reports reaching him that the Jacobite main body had moved off westwards, William, however uncharacteristically, must have felt a surge of elation: barring unforeseen catastrophe, victory was his for the taking. Orders were issued for the army centre to begin its advance via King William's Glen, whilst he would take the reserve on a longer, more circuitous route behind the ridgeline north of Tullyallen in order to swing round and link up with Ginkel somewhere between Drybridge and Mill Ford.

Led by the *Gardes te Voet*, the Williamite foot moved further into the defile, slowly being swallowed up by the last lingering traces of early morning mist which still clung to the valley floor, and as the path veered south towards Oldbridge, the column divided. The Dutch Guards continuing further towards the river for a short distance before halting and awaiting the order to attack. The remainder of the column, led by the Duke of Schomberg, struck out across the high ground to the east of King William's Glen, heading towards the fords at Grove and Yellow islands.

Regrettably there is no eyewitness account of how the Williamite centre moved into position prior to its attack. However, given the known timings of when the units became engaged, the most likely explanation is that the leading unit – de la Melonière's Huguenot battalion – almost immediately peeled off from the line of march to face southwards towards the river before continuing its advance, and that each successive unit in the line of march – Caillemotte's, Cambon's and Hanmer's – peeled off in sequence, thereby creating the echeloned line of attack that eventually stretched from King William's Glen to Yellow Island.

On the opposite side of the valley, Tyrconnel was in a quandary: his orders were to prepare for a withdrawal, but a large number of enemy

The Boyne at Oldbridge, looking southwards to the *Gardes te Voet's* crossing point. After leaving King William's Glen, the *Gardes te Voet* formed three assault columns before moving across the river to assault the Jacobite garrison of Oldbridge. (Author's photograph)

troops had appeared from nowhere and were now advancing towards him in full view. Accordingly, he ordered Lieutenant General Richard Hamilton to move towards the river with both battalions of King James's Foot Guards under an Englishman, Colonel William Dorrington, with the Earl of Antrim's regiment of foot in support. The two-battalion regiment of the Marquis de Boisseleau – the least experienced but also the best equipped of Hamilton's troops – then moved forward to cover his original position.

With the exception of Clanrickarde's regiment in Oldbridge and the three regiments under the command of Lord Iveagh which were garrisoning Drogheda, these five battalions – roughly 3,000 men – are believed to have represented Tyrconnel's entire infantry strength. The clue to this apparent discrepancy again lies in Laisné's correspondence with the French war ministry, in which he states that Tyrconnel's second line of troops consisted of two regiments of dragoons – which we know to have been commanded by Lord Dongan and Viscount Clare – and a single battalion of foot which he calls 'Baguenette'. Given the problem that the French had with the transcription of Irish names (the Duke of Berwick has 16 different variations of his name, whilst Tyrconnel himself has nine), it would be tempting to identify this mystery regiment as that of Colonel Dudley Bagenal (which we know was present at the Cookstown review on 24 June), but the whereabouts of this unit during the battle are uncorroborated elsewhere, in addition to which, as the fighting around Oldbridge intensified, it is difficult to assume that Tyrconnel would have left any available units uncommitted.

ABOVE OLDBRIDGE

Following his decision to bring the main body of his army after de Lauzun, James issued orders that the remainder of the artillery should also withdraw from the field in the wake of the baggage train. This meant

The Battle of the Boyne (VS2841). The artist has combined several events from the battle without regard to time or distance: in the foreground, Count Schomberg attacks the Jacobites at 'the bridge of Slane', whilst in the centre a senior officer – presumably William – directs the battle. In the background, Williamite columns ford the river to attack Oldbridge. (With kind permission of the Trustees, Atlas Van Stolk, Rotterdam)

that at the crucial moment, Tyrconnel would have no artillery support whatsoever. Although William's forces around Oldbridge would enjoy total artillery superiority, the presence of one or two Jacobite guns, even though their loss would have been likely, could have had a devastating effect upon the Williamite troops as they emerged from the water.

Again, in his letter to Louvois, dated 8 July, Laisné maintains that on the evening prior to the battle he had deployed two batteries of artillery to cover the crossings at Oldbridge: the first under Desvaux consisting of five cannon deployed to cover the left-hand side of the village, whilst three guns under d'Agincourt were placed to defend the right hand side. He then states that when the Williamite cannon deployed on the ridgeline to the west of Tullyallen opened fire early on the morning of the battle, their shot fell not only amongst the defenders of Oldbridge but also in the Jacobite artillery park, and that it was because of this that the batteries were withdrawn from the vicinity of Oldbridge, and the park itself moved.

An important point to note is that these guns and their crews were all French, and again the spectre of Louvois rears its head – did the withdrawal take place out of concern for their loss to the army, or was it based upon instructions from Versailles?

Laisné insists that he received his orders from Richard Hamilton, who, in turn, had received them from one of James's aides, and maintains that he withdrew Desvaux's battery first as it was the more exposed – lying directly in the Williamite gunners' line of fire, and then d'Agincourt – thereafter pulling back along the road to Duleek where they would join the confusion of the Jacobite retreat through the bottleneck.

KING WILLIAM'S GLEN

At a little before 9.00am, and just as the early morning mist began to dissipate in the valley floor, the signal was given for the Williamite artillery deployed on the ridge below Tullyallen to open fire. Consisting of three batteries of field guns and one of mortars, they initially opened fire both on the Jacobite positions around Oldbridge and the artillery park on the Hill of Donore. When James ordered his artillery back, out of range and therefore to all intents and purposes out of the battle, they began to concentrate their fire upon Clanrickarde's regiment, which the previous day had entrenched itself in and around Oldbridge.

For almost an hour the bombardment continued to soften up the Jacobite position, apparently causing few casualties, but certainly causing the defenders severe discomfort – demoralizing them and ensuring that they kept their heads down. Then, shortly after 10.00am, the bombardment ceased and the echoes of gunfire were replaced by a short staccato drumbeat as the *Gardes te Voet* debouched from King William's Glen to assault Clanrickarde's position. To the tune of the popular doggerel lillibulero, the Dutchmen left the defile, forming up into three ten-man-wide assault columns, spearheaded by their grenadier companies, generally the fittest and toughest men in the regiment. At the council of war, Solms had boasted that his men would sweep the Irish and their French allies from the field, and that is what he intended to do.

Halberd, possibly French, late 17th century. With the same usage as the partizan, the halberd was used by NCOs or colour guards. (Photograph courtesy of the Trustees, Royal Armouries, Leeds)

Oldbridge – the initial Jacobite infantry positions. With the exception of the Oldbridge garrison, Tyrconnel's infantry were deployed behind this ridge and moved downhill to counter Schomberg's advance, seemingly 'rising out of the ground'. (Author's photograph)

Grove Island – the Huguenot's crossing point. A small boggy islet in the Boyne, Grove Island provided the springboard for William's second attack as de la Melonière's Huguenot regiment plunged into the water followed by Caillemotte's and du Cambon's. (Author's photograph)

Plunging into the river, William's Guards began to splash across the shallows and soon came under fire from the Irish troops in Oldbridge, but the range was too great and the fire ineffective. Diverging, the three battalions began to move on the Jacobite defences from both front and flanks, and as they clambered up onto the southern bank many of them must have given a momentary vote of thanks to their comrades manning the guns on the ridgeline above, fully aware of what their own fate would have been had the two French batteries not been forced to withdraw from their positions on either side of the village.

Fanning out, the Blue Guards went over to the attack, and for almost a quarter of an hour were held at bay, having to clear individual positions at bayonet point. Slowly, albeit grudgingly, Clanrickarde's men were forced out of their defences and into the cornfields that lay outside the village, exchanging volleys with the enemy – the Irishmen equipped with outdated and slow-firing matchlock muskets or pikes competing with an enemy armed with modern flintlocks and socket bayonets, where each

The Boyne – looking towards Yellow Island, the Danes' crossing point. Once the Danes had established William's third bridgehead across the river and stretched the Jacobite infantry to breaking point, it remained to the Irish cavalry to stem the attacking tide. (Author's photograph)

soldier was a musketeer or pikeman in equal measure. The Jacobite army was organized in a ratio of roughly two musketeers for every pikeman, effectively meaning that roughly two-thirds of Clanrickarde's regiment would have been equipped with firearms of some description, whilst in the *Gardes te Voet* all 'other ranks' would have had a musket and bayonet, thereby putting out a weight of fire – even without taking misfires into account – of over three times that of the Irishmen.

In the army review that King James held on 1–2 October 1689, and as was reported by the French commissary Fumeron, the Earl of Clanrickarde's regiment of foot consisted of 36 officers, 26 NCOs and 694 other ranks. Of the latter, 436 were armed with serviceable firearms, 201 with pike or half pike and (at that time) 44 were unarmed. The remainder were the regimental drummers, of which each company had one.

East of Oldbridge, Richard Hamilton was deployed with three battalions of Jacobite foot in order to repulse any attack that may have been made by the enemy troops that were currently descending towards Grove and Yellow islands. However, rightly believing that the Dutch Guards' attack posed the most serious and immediate threat to the Jacobite position and leaving the Earl of Antrim's regiment of foot to cover the two islands, Hamilton ordered Dorrington forward with the two battalions of Irish Guards in a swift and spirited counter-attack.

In closing with the Dutch Guards, Major Thomas Arthur of the 1st battalion 'ran the officer through the body that commanded the Battalion he marched up to, before sustaining a mortal wound', and after an initial flurry of hand-to-hand combat, a firefight ensued with the remnants of Clanrickarde's regiment falling in on the left flank of the Irish Guards. Again, Dutch fire discipline proved too much for the Jacobites and, despite their stubborn defiance, the Irishmen were pushed back, continually re-forming and re-engaging the Williamite foot, conceding ground but refusing to concede victory to the enemy.

After roughly half an hour of intense combat, and as the *Gardes te Voet* began to clear Oldbridge and consolidate their position there, Hamilton threw in his last infantry unit in an attempt to tip the balance and retrieve the situation. Alexandre de Rainier de Droué, Marquis de Boisseleau, commanded a two-battalion regiment of foot that would have mustered well over a thousand men at the Boyne. Although it was not Hamilton's most experienced formation, it was probably his best equipped on account of a period spent as part of the Cork garrison, which allowed de Boisseleau to equip his men straight from the incoming French convoys rather than to indent the quartermaster general for supplies from the army's magazines. Accordingly a higher proportion of the troops were armed with firearms than in the rest of the Jacobite army.

GROVE ISLAND

As the Jacobite Foot Guards moved forward against their Dutch counterparts engaged around Oldbridge the leading regiment of William's Huguenot brigade, that of Colonel de la Melonière, reached the river to the west of Grove Island and began to cross. Immediately the problems of crossing a tidal river became apparent – the three battalions of Dutch Guards had effectively dammed the river whilst they were making their way across, and now this water was released downstream, making the Frenchmen's crossing that much more difficult. Their presence, however, threw the Jacobite counter-attack off balance and the advance faltered, instinctively pulling away from the river and towards their original positions on the ridgeline. Officers attempted to spur their men on for one last charge – de Boisseleau later wrote to his wife that he tried three times to get his men to close with the enemy, but to no avail.

These were not, however, the 'mob of cowstealers' described by Macaulay in his *History of England*, who 'flung away arms, colours, and cloaks, and scampered off to the hills without striking a blow or firing a shot'; they were a force of men who, in what was for many their first major battle, had been in combat with arguably the finest infantry in Europe and had come through bloodied but unbowed.

On top of the ridge overlooking the southern bank of the Boyne, Tyrconnel could see that the situation was worsening. It was now approaching 11.30am and in the preceding hour and a half Clanrickarde had been ejected from Oldbridge and, with the exception of Antrim's foot, who were still lining the riverbank between the two islands, his whole infantry force was being slowly but inexorably pushed away from the river. Along the northern bank, increasing numbers of enemy troops began to file into the water, the Jacobite position deteriorating with every passing minute.

To retrieve the situation, he launched arguably his best regiments – King James's Life Guards and his own regiment of horse – against the *Gardes te Voet*, who had by now halted to the south and east of Oldbridge and were re-forming. Led by Lieutenant Colonel Dominic Sheldon and the 19-year-old Duke of Berwick, the Jacobite horsemen thundered downhill, slowly gathering speed and momentum as they approached the Dutchmen. As the range closed and the Irishmen rode through the pall of smoke that lay on the battlefield, the Dutch Guards presented muskets and opened fire.

Observing the charge, William is reputed to have held his breath, fearing that his guards would be ridden down, but the close-range volley disordered the Jacobite horse and, unable to close, they turned and rode back to their start positions to rally and re-form.

It was now almost midday, and as more Williamite regiments reached the river, the Duke of Schomberg began to cross at the head of his small staff; behind him Caillemotte's, Cambon's and Hanmer's regiments all floundered in the chest-deep water, whilst to their rear and unable to cross behind the Huguenots, a brigade of Ulster Protestants turned upstream in order to ford the Boyne at Oldbridge, which was now relatively clear. Whilst the bulk of the troops crossed behind the Dutch Guards, St John's Londonderry regiment began to form up on their left flank, continuing their line to the river.

In front of the Williamite centre, Antrim's regiment fired a few desultory volleys to little effect, and as Hamilton rode up to lead them against the oncoming enemy it was simply too much: unsupported by the rest of their brigade which was by now retreating towards the Hill of Donore, and with William's Anglo-Dutch and Danish brigades extending well beyond their right flank, the Jacobite regiment recoiled and joined in the retreat. His brigade shattered, Hamilton rode up to Tyrconnel's command post where the Jacobite horse was forming up for another charge and attached himself to one of Parker's squadrons.

ROUGHGRANGE

Consolidating his position on the southern bank of the Boyne, Meinhard Schomberg advanced cautiously against what he perceived to be the Jacobite left flank, which gave James Douglas time to catch him up and add his five battalions to the flanking column, bringing it up to approximately 11,000 men. The slowness of Count Schomberg's advance gave de Lauzun the time needed to bring his wing up to Roughgrange by about 10.30am and deploy into line of battle on one side of a ravine, thereby blocking the Williamites' line of advance.

Although de Lauzun had the smaller force and was inferior in cavalry, with Montgrizy's battery he had parity in artillery, and there was no real comparison between his French veterans and Schomberg's infantry, many of whom had only been under arms for a matter of months. By late morning, couriers came from James's headquarters advising of the arrival of the main body of the army, and as the number of Jacobite troops facing Count Schomberg doubled, the Jacobite left wing sidestepped to the left in order to let the new arrivals deploy for action.

As has been said, James, believing that Count Schomberg commanded the leading element of William's main force, was impatient to come to grips with what he perceived to be a lesser force, and his impatience soon transferred itself to his troops, who, seeing an inferior enemy body in front of them, cried out for the order to attack to be given. It was now, at about midday, that a courier from Tyrconnel reached James advising him that William's army had forced a crossing at Oldbridge and that he was attempting to contain the enemy forces.

Ordering his dragoons to dismount and screen the advance of the army, James gave the order to attack before word of Tyrconnel's situation became common knowledge. But soon word came back from Colonels Patrick Sarsfield and Thomas Maxwell, riding in front of the army, that the ravine itself was boggy and that local drainage ditches would prohibit any form of a frontal attack by the Jacobites.

The Battle of the Boyne by Romeyn de Hooghe. One of the more famous images of the battle shows the Duke of Schomberg cut down whilst surrounded by a knot of Jacobite horsemen. Behind the Duke, large columns of Williamite infantry force their way across the river into the hamlet of Oldbridge. (Collection Ulster Museum Belfast, courtesy Trustees NMGNI)

Across the ravine, Meinhard Schomberg must have received much the same news from his own scouts, as his troops then turned to their right and marched to the south, as if seeking a way around the obstacle, but also moving dangerously closer to the Jacobite rear. Matching the Williamites, and led again by de Lauzun's Frenchmen, James's army turned to its left and began to march off, this time for Duleek, the bottleneck over the river Nanny, upon which the Jacobite army's line of communication with Dublin depended.

As the Franco-Irish troops set off, rumours started to circulate about events at Oldbridge and then the Williamite cavalry began to snipe at the column with carbine fire. A sense of urgency developed as the troops began to feel themselves being caught within an enemy pincer movement rather than by the harassment of an isolated body of troops.

THE JACOBITE HIGH-WATER MARK

After their abortive charge upon the *Gardes te Voet*, the Life Guards and Tyrconnel's regiment quickly rallied and this time, accompanied by John Parker's regiment of horse, they thundered back downhill towards the enemy forces now clambering up the southern bank of the Boyne.

As they approached the river, the troopers turned to their left and rode through the leading elements of several Williamite regiments. Whether they had been halted by Antrim's ineffectual presence or simply delayed by the hazardous crossing is unclear, although the Danish account of the battle states that until its flank was threatened by the crossing at Yellow Island, the Jacobite regiment had successfully prevented the Williamite centre from advancing. Parker's horse thundered through the front ranks of Sir John Hanmer's English foot whilst the Life Guards and Tyrconnel's troopers smashed into the leading elements of Caillemotte's Huguenot regiment, mortally wounding Caillemotte himself.

Slightly ahead of the Huguenot foot, the Duke of Schomberg vainly tried to rally them as the wave of enemy horsemen engulfed his small

75

Oldbridge – view from behind the Jacobite cavalry positions. Once the order to attack had been given, the Jacobite horse swept down from this ridge several times into the enemy ranks, with varying success. The reckless nature of their attacks gained them praise from friend and foe alike, establishing their reputation as being the equal of the best cavalry in Europe. (Author's photograph)

party, and, as the Jacobite charge rolled on, Schomberg and his aides were left dead or dying. There is uncertainty about who actually struck the blow that killed the Duke – Jacobite sources would suggest either a Lifeguard named Brian O'Toole or Sir Charles Take (or Tuke), an Englishman who was serving as a volunteer in Tyrconnel's regiment, whilst Williamite sources intimate that the Duke was killed by a chance shot fired by one of the Huguenot infantry as he emerged from the river: 'One master Bryen O'Tool of the guards, discovering his former acquaintance, marshal Schomberg, near the village of Oldbridge, resolved to sacrifice his life to the making him away, upon which he, with a few of the guards, and a few of Tyrconnel's horse made up to him, and O'Tool with his pistol shot the marshal dead.'

Schomberg and Caillemotte were not the only casualties of note: the Reverend George Walker, one-time joint-governor of Londonderry, had inexplicably attached himself to Caillemotte's regiment when the Ulster foot moved upstream to cross the Boyne at Oldbridge. As the Jacobite horse fell upon the Huguenot foot, Walker was shot in the stomach and died in the shallows. The two soldiers would be deeply mourned, but reaction to Walker's fate can be summed up in William's own words 'The fool! What business had he there?'

Cutting through the leading elements of de la Melonière's regiment, the bulk of the Jacobite horse continued forward and swept into St John's infantry who were caught changing formation from column to line. The bulk of the cavalry were able to rein in and pull back towards their original position where they re-formed for another charge, but a number of riders were unable to halt their momentum and carried on upstream where they were apparently surrounded and killed.

Irrespective of who was responsible for inflicting Schomberg's fatal wound, the situation in the Williamite centre was now critical. Without leadership the disordered troops could neither advance nor retreat and they could look for no immediate support as the Dutch Guards were reorganizing and consolidating their position, whilst the Danes had yet to cross the river.

The Jacobite horse regrouped and, as the Danes crossed further downstream, made a penultimate attempt to break the Dutch Guards around Oldbridge, but again the attack was foiled by the discipline and firepower of the Dutchmen. Closing to within pistol range, a few troopers fired on the enemy foot, and then the mass of cavalry withdrew once more.

YELLOW ISLAND

With the Jacobite foot in retreat, and the majority of Tyrconnel's mounted troops engaged against the Huguenot brigade, the Danish troops under Württemberg-Neustadt were able to make their crossing virtually unopposed. It was not an easy crossing, however, as the water was deep and the riverbed treacherous underfoot. Fearing that they might drown, many of the soldiers simply froze in the water but eventually, carrying their arms and ammunition above their heads and spearheaded by King Christian's Foot Guards and several companies of grenadiers, the Danes were able to establish a fragile presence on the southern bank – the Duke himself being carried across on his grenadiers' shoulders.

Reacting swiftly, Tyrconnel released virtually his last uncommitted troops – the dragoon regiments of Walter, Lord Dongan and Charles O'Brien, Viscount Clare – to halt the Danes and prevent them from consolidating their position. It was several hundred against several thousand and, unlike O'Neill's troops at Rossnaree, both regiments fought mounted. Closing with the Danish infantry, O'Brien's regiment rode straight into a Danish volley and was driven off, whilst Dongan's found itself facing a regiment of Danish cavalry.

Unlike the Danish foot, the Danish horse had been raised specifically to serve in Ireland and were among the most inexperienced troops in William's army. It was an uneven contest and Dongan's men scattered their opponents sending them fleeing across the river. As the Irishmen turned about to ascend the hill once more and re-form for another attack, tragedy struck – Dongan was struck by a Williamite shot and killed. Demoralized, both Jacobite units began to pull back towards Donore in disorder. They had, however, achieved their objective – without mounted support, the Danish infantry were pinned against the river and could only try to maintain their position in the face of the hitherto unchallenged Jacobite cavalry.

WILLIAM CROSSES THE BOYNE

Originally intending to cross the Boyne almost simultaneously with Solms's *Gardes te Voet*, Ginkel's cavalry column almost immediately ran into difficulty: the river at Mill Ford was deep and, once across, any attacking force would be disadvantaged by having to contend with the steeply ascending southern bank. With Tyrconnel's reserves as yet uncommitted, he had no realistic option other than to hold his position until the situation on the centre and right flanks developed and the Jacobites were drawn into combat elsewhere.

As soon as he saw the failure of the Jacobite horse to break the *Gardes te Voet*, William and his staff rode towards Drybridge in order to catch up with the army's left wing and, as he joined the column, a courier brought news of the Jacobites' devastating charge against the army centre and the deaths of Schomberg, Caillemotte and (presumably) Walker.

THE DEATH OF THE DUKE OF SCHOMBERG, 1 JULY 1690
(Pages 78–79)

Following the successful lodgement at Oldbridge by the Dutch *Gardes te Voet* under Solms, the second phase of the Williamite attack began to develop with the crossing of Huguenot and Anglo-Dutch troops under the Duke of Schomberg at Grove Island, some 200m further downstream. With a small escort, Schomberg (1) had crossed in advance of the infantry, and is shown here wearing the red statecoat of a Brandenburg general with the sash and insignia of the Order of the Garter, awarded to him by King William III. The duke remained an officer in the Brandenburg army, and was fighting for William with the permission of the Elector. As a sign of his service to William, he is wearing an orange waist sash. As the Williamite foot (2) began to clamber out onto the southern bank, Tyrconnel launched three cavalry regiments into the attack, smashing into the disorganized infantry as they tried to form up, and breaking into Sir John Hanmer's, Caillemotte's and de la Melonière's regiments in turn before continuing downstream. Here we see the Duke of Schomberg's party surrounded by a wave of King James's Life Guards as he tries to rally his broken infantrymen (3). These men are from the 2nd troop of Guards, (commanded by King James's son, the Duke of Berwick), as shown by their green hat ribbons, carbine slings and saddle furniture. Behind the duke, we see one Jacobite horseman, alternately credited as being either Brian O'Toole or Sir Charles Take (4), about to fire what is believed to have been the fatal shot which killed Schomberg. In the rear of the picture, one of Schomberg's aides (5) is vainly attempting to come to his commander's rescue. (Graham Turner)

The Battle of the Boyne by Jan Wyck. This sketch bears a more than passing resemblance to that by Theodor Maas, as both are drawn from the artillery positions at Tullyallen, with the infantry attacks taking place in the centre and background of the drawing. Wyck differs in that he also places William's senior officers in the image, although most of them were at the time in different parts of the battlefield. (Photograph courtesy of the National Gallery of Ireland, Dublin)

Determined to break the impasse, William seized the opportunity offered by the fact that the enemy were fixated on engaging the infantry pinned against the Boyne or defending Oldbridge, and some time around 12.15pm he ordered his cavalry across. Closest to the river, Ginkel's troops led the way, brushing aside a mounted Jacobite piquet, and followed by the reserve cavalry: the passage of so many horses made the ford impassable for foot units, and so William was obliged to send his infantry reserve back upstream in order to attempt a crossing.

Following in Ginkel's wake, William's mount soon got into severe difficulty, becoming mired in the churned-up riverbed. Dismounting, the King attempted to lead his horse across the river. This would have been arduous enough for someone of strong constitution, but for the delicate William it was almost fatal, as he succumbed to a severe asthma attack. Gasping for breath, he could have drowned but was rescued by an Enniskillen trooper named McKinlay, who unceremoniously dragged him and his mount to firmer ground on the southern bank.

William's crossing was the Jacobite death knell: as soon as the fleeing piquets reported the presence of a substantial body of enemy cavalry on the south bank of the river, Tyrconnel knew that it was the end. Outnumbered and outgunned, his sole advantage had been the lack of enemy cavalry on the field, and now in one fell swoop this superiority has been erased. The only option now would be to attempt a fighting withdrawal before the Williamites could reorganize and coordinate their forces, and rejoin the rest of the army. Turning to an aide, he penned a laconic message to his sovereign: 'The Enemy has forced the river, the Right Wing is defeated.' It was a quarter to one in the afternoon, and the fighting had by now lasted almost three hours from when the Dutch Guards waded across the river Boyne.

THE FORLORN HOPE

Almost a kilometre behind Tyrconnel's position, the Duleek road is dominated by Donore graveyard. A walled enclosure built upon a steep hill, it was a perfect position from which the Jacobites could ambush enemy pursuers and halt them long enough for the remnants of the right wing to escape. And so having garrisoned the enclosure with a

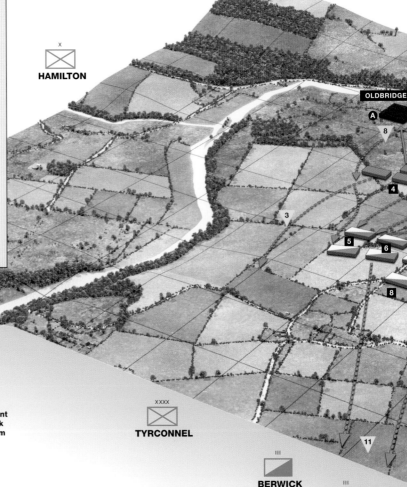

WILLIAMITES

A *Gardes te Voet* (Dutch – three battalions and attached cadets)

B De la Melonière's Regiment of Foot (Huguenot – one battalion)

C Caillemotte's Regiment of Foot (Huguenot – one battalion)

D Cambon's Regiment of Foot (Huguenot – one battalion)

E Sir John Hanmer's Regiment of Foot (English – one battalion)

F Nassau-Saarbrücken-Ottweiler Regiment of Foot (Dutch – one battalion)

G Brandenburg Regiment of Foot (Dutch – one battalion)

H Artillery Train

I Colonel John Mitchelbourne's Regiment of Foot (Londonderry – one battalion)

J Colonel Thomas St John's Regiment of Foot (Londonderry – one battalion)

K Lord George Hamilton's Regiment of Foot (Enniskillen – one battalion)

L Colonel Zachariah Tiffin's Regiment of Foot (Enniskillen – one battalion)

M Danish Brigade (eight foot battalions, three horse regiments)

N Williamite left wing (three regiments of horse, three regiments of dragoons, 10 battalions of foot)

O Lt. Gen. Ginkel's Brigade (six cavalry regiments)

HAMILTON

OLDBRIDGE

TYRCONNEL

BERWICK

SHELDON

▼ EVENTS

1. 11.30AM **Tyrconnel orders his own regiment (6) and King James's Life Guards (5) to attack the Dutch *Gardes te Voet* (A) debouching from Oldbridge.**

2. 11.30AM **The Danish Brigade (M) under Württemburg begins to cross the Boyne at Yellow Island.**

3. 11.30AM **The Irish foot withdraw southwards towards the Hill of Donore.**

4. 11.40AM **The Dutch beat off Tyrconnel's attack, with the Jacobites retiring to the ridgeline to reform.**

5. 11.55AM **The Jacobite cavalry launches another attack with the Life Guards (5) under Berwick, Tyrconnel's horse (6) under Sheldon, and Parker's horse (8) temporarily under the command of Richard Hamilton. The Jacobites sweep along the riverbank breaking into several Williamite regiments as they emerge from the river – Hanmer's (E), Caillemotte's (C), de la Melonière's (B) and St. John's (J) who are forming up on the left flank of the Dutch *Gardes te Voet* (A). During the confused and running mêlée, the Duke of Schomberg's staff is overrun and the Duke is killed. The Huguenot colonel, Caillemotte, is also mortally wounded.**

6. 11.55AM **Tyrconnel's two dragoon regiments – Dongan's (9) and Clare's (10) – are successfully sent to dispute the Danish crossing, but Dongan is killed as his regiment withdraws to reform for another attack.**

7. 12.15PM **The Williamite left wing (N) begins to cross the Boyne at Mill Ford, south of Drybridge, turning the Jacobite right flank.**

8. 12.20PM **Having re-formed his troops, Tyrconnel orders his cavalry to once more charge the Dutch *Gardes te Voet* (A). Unable to close due to a combination of adverse terrain and Dutch firepower, the Jacobites again withdraw to reform on the ridge.**

9. 12.45PM **Severely outnumbered, with his right flank turned and virtually no reserves, Tyrconnel orders his forces to withdraw towards the Hill of Donore.**

10. 1.15PM **Leading elements of Williamite left wing (N) begin to advance from Mill Ford towards the Hill of Donore.**

11. 1.30PM **Withdrawing from the field, the Jacobites re-form, twice mounting rearguard actions at Donore Graveyard and Platin Hall, where Richard Hamilton is captured. this delays William's forces sufficiently to enable the Jacobites to disengage and cross the Nanny at Duleek.**

THE JACOBITE COLLAPSE

1 July 1690, viewed looking north to south (and vice-versa), showing the Jacobite counter-attacks against the initial Williamite bridgeheads across the Boyne and their response to the subsequent crossings at Yellow Island and Drybridge, leading to the eventual collapse of the defensive line and retreat to the Hill of Donore.

Note: Gridlines are shown at intervals of 250m

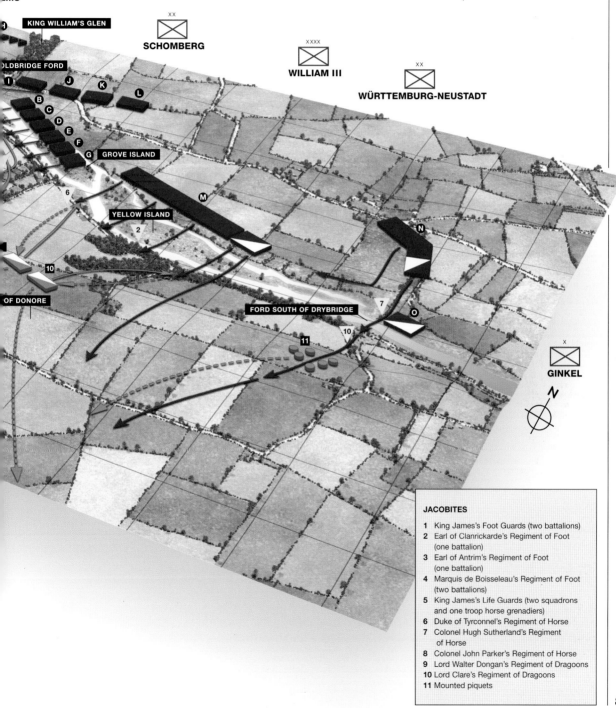

MS

KING WILLIAM'S GLEN

SCHOMBERG

WILLIAM III

WÜRTTEMBURG-NEUSTADT

OLDBRIDGE FORD

I J K L
B
C
D
E
F
G GROVE ISLAND

YELLOW ISLAND

M

N

O

OF DONORE

FORD SOUTH OF DRYBRIDGE

GINKEL

N

JACOBITES

1 King James's Foot Guards (two battalions)
2 Earl of Clanrickarde's Regiment of Foot
  (one battalion)
3 Earl of Antrim's Regiment of Foot
  (one battalion)
4 Marquis de Boisseleau's Regiment of Foot
  (two battalions)
5 King James's Life Guards (two squadrons
  and one troop horse grenadiers)
6 Duke of Tyrconnel's Regiment of Horse
7 Colonel Hugh Sutherland's Regiment
  of Horse
8 Colonel John Parker's Regiment of Horse
9 Lord Walter Dongan's Regiment of Dragoons
10 Lord Clare's Regiment of Dragoons
11 Mounted piquets

Oldbridge, looking south towards the Hill of Donore. Following their collapse, the Jacobite infantry fell back along this route in various stages of disorder, with many not stopping even after they reached Duleek. (Author's photograph)

mixture of dismounted horse and dragoons and possibly some stragglers from Hamilton's infantry, they formed up in the fields a short distance behind the improvised redoubt and grimly waited for the enemy to appear.

Having ascended the slopes south of Mill Ford unopposed, the Williamite cavalry led by William and Ginkel rode off in pursuit of the retreating enemy, but as they approached the graveyard chaos ensued. Inside the walls, the dismounted Jacobites kept up a heavy fire on the approaching horsemen, but the walls were not built for defence, and soon the two forces were intermingled with small, local firefights and mêlées taking place.

Riding up at the head of a force comprising Wolseley's Enniskilleners and the Duke of Schomberg's horse, William sought to break the enemy troopers positioned south of the graveyard, but the enclosed terrain and the attackers' numerical superiority soon began to work against him – Tyrconnel's Irishmen knew where the enemy was and who he was, but amid the smoke and din of battle, for William's multinational and multilingual force it was another matter entirely, with friend being taken for foe at a moment's notice. In the confusion of close combat, the Enniskilleners reputedly charged Donop's white-coated Danish cavalry, having mistaken them for a Jacobite regiment, possibly Parker's or Sutherland's. William himself courted death for the third or fourth time that day when an Enniskillen trooper pulled a pistol on him and was barely restrained from pulling the trigger.

Ginkel then attempted to outflank the western side of the Jacobite position but was soon beaten back by a unit of enemy cavalry and, as both bodies mingled in close combat, they were fired upon by some English dragoons who had deployed themselves along the hedgerows.

The more troops that William threw into the mêlée, the worse the problems of command and control became. Tyrconnel had turned and given his pursuers a bloody nose – there is no record of Jacobite losses, but those on the Williamite side numbered around 150 dead and wounded, equal to some 5 per cent of the force that had crossed at Mill Ford – and was now able to disengage southwards.

PLATIN: THE FINAL STAND

Once more the race was on between pursuers and pursued, and again, the Jacobites turned to face their attackers. In an attempt to block the road, Richard Hamilton placed a body of horse drawn from the various regiments in an enclosed field near Platin Hall, whose only entrance was along a narrow double-banked lane which ran from east to west in front of the field and then north to south along its western side.

The Enniskillen horse were maintaining their position at the forefront of the Williamite advance and, as their leading troops approached Hamilton's position, Wolseley mistakenly gave the order to 'wheel to the left', resulting in his troops presenting their rear to the waiting Jacobites. The order was immediately countermanded, but it was too late: in the confusion, Hamilton charged and broke the Ulstermen, killing or wounding around 50 of their number.

Having routed Wolseley's troops, Hamilton overreached himself by pursuing the enemy, and rode straight into the mass of horsemen being led by William towards Duleek. Severely outnumbered, the Irishmen were simply overwhelmed and scattered in all directions. Hamilton, wounded, was brought before the king.

Looking down at the man whom he saw as being responsible for the war, William asked if Hamilton thought that the Jacobites would stand and fight again. 'Upon my Honour, I believe they will,' replied the prisoner. 'Your Honour? Upon your Honour?' said William sarcastically, and ordered Hamilton to be led away into captivity.

THE BRIDGE AT DULEEK

As they marched along the Duleek road, the situation in the Jacobite army was anything but the model of military efficiency. It is true that aggressive mounted patrols were lessening the effect of the enemy horsemen, but the force was fragmenting from within: the senior officers had tended to

congregate around James's headquarters, which ordinarily would have caused no real problems, but here there were no plans, no orders given, merely a subconscious need to reach Duleek. Furthermore, there was a small riot when some men broke ranks and smashed open barrels of spirits and proceeded, in a number of cases, to become very drunk. Fuel was added to the fire with the rumours that were filtering through about events at Oldbridge. Then, some time between 12.30pm and 12.45pm came Tyrconnel's bombshell: the right wing had been defeated at Oldbridge and was in retreat.

Fearful for James's safety, and with the King's bodyguard engaged on the right wing, de Lauzun immediately detailed Sarsfield's Horse and Maxwell's Dragoons to escort the King from the field and to safety. By reducing his mounted reserve to just two regiments of horse (Abercorn's and Galmoy's) and two of dragoons (Clifford's and Carroll's), this overreaction on the Frenchman's part crippled the army by weakening its ability to undertake any real action against the Williamite cavalry which was nipping at the column's flanks and rear. There was now only one concern that occupied the Jacobites: to reach Duleek and cross the Magdalene Bridge over the river Nanny to safety.

On the road from Duleek to Donore all was chaos, with scattered groups of Jacobites, both mounted and dismounted, many having thrown away their arms and equipment and even coats and shoes to gain that little bit more speed, fleeing in an attempt to outdistance the Williamite pursuit. On the road, Laisné's batteries were overrun by the remnants of the Clare dragoons, but in the time that it took for the fugitives to extricate themselves from the confusion, Charles O'Brien was able to rally a few dozen of his men who, in the coming weeks, would serve as the guns' escort all the way to the walls of Limerick.

Miraculously de Lauzun managed to get his forces to Duleek without incident, but then disaster struck. Led by the Duke of Berwick, a number of cavalry fleeing from Platin Hall rode straight into the tightly packed ranks of infantry waiting to cross the Duleek Bridge. The Grand Prior's Regiment, commanded by another of James's sons, Henry Fitzjames, was part of Wauchope's brigade, and one of its officers, John Stevens, described the scene as follows:

For the horse in general, taking their flight towards the left, broke the whole line of foot, riding over all our battalions … The horse came on so unexpected and at such speed, some firing their pistols, that we had no time to receive them, but all supposing them to be the enemy (as indeed they were no better to us) took to their heels, no officer being able to stop the men after they were broken, and the horse past, though at the same time no enemy was near us or them that fled in such haste to our destruction

The picture is clear: there was no real organized pursuit at this stage. Although he was continually harassing the enemy columns, Count Schomberg lacked the strength to mount a major attack on the Jacobites, whilst at Oldbridge, the Williamites under Solms and Württemberg-Neustadt were reorganizing after over three hours of intense combat. And with the reserve infantry still in the process of crossing the Boyne, the only force capable of mounting a serious pursuit of the enemy was William's left-wing cavalry, which had been twice bloodied when the Jacobites had turned at Donore graveyard and Platin Hall; there was no 'golden bridge' that William left open to prevent his father-in-law from being captured by his forces a second time. Simply put, for an hour or two, William's army was incapable of pursuit, although the fact was unknown to James's troops attempting to escape across the river at Duleek.

The Magdalene Bridge across the Nanny was a very narrow construction, across which it was reckoned that fewer than six men could march abreast, whilst the riverbanks were steep and boggy, thus creating the bottleneck that almost trapped the Jacobite army. With the mounted regiments positioned to hold off any advancing Williamite troops, the Jacobite foot and artillery began to cross. As time passed and more and more men filed across the stone arches, it looked as if de Lauzun might be able to extricate the entire army, but it was at this point that Berwick's mounted fugitives collided with Wauchope's brigade.

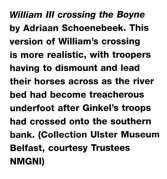

William III crossing the Boyne by Adriaan Schoenebeek. This version of William's crossing is more realistic, with troopers having to dismount and lead their horses across as the river bed had become treacherous underfoot after Ginkel's troops had crossed onto the southern bank. (Collection Ulster Museum Belfast, courtesy Trustees NMGNI)

The Magdalene Bridge at Duleek. After both Jacobite wings had begun to withdraw, the army's survival came down to who could reach the bridge first. Wide enough to take six men marching abreast, the bridge formed a bottleneck that could have resulted in the destruction of the Jacobite army had the Williamites been able to mount a serious pursuit. (Author's photograph)

At about 5.00pm, the mounted rearguard eventually turned and crossed the river, dogged by Count Schomberg's leading elements, and followed the main column cross-country to the main Dublin road. Without waiting for further instructions, Schomberg set out in pursuit, pressing the Jacobite rearguard (now comprising the French Brigade) so hard that they were obliged to halt and deploy for battle, and a long-range firefight ensued. Casualties were light, and the French battalions leapfrogged back for about three miles, where they had to ford another river, the Naul.

Drawn up on the southern bank of this river, Tyrconnel had deployed several battalions of foot and as much cavalry as he could muster into a defensive formation. The French troops now crossed the river and for the next few hours both sides glowered at each other across the Naul until about approximately 10.00pm when William issued orders for Schomberg to halt the pursuit.

James had made his gesture in the defence of Dublin and, despite the courage and tenacity of Tyrconnel's wing and de Lauzun's skill in bringing the bulk of the army intact from the field, the campaign had been a disaster. Losses in manpower had not been great but the equipment which was being collected all across the Hill of Donore and in the lanes around Duleek was of critical importance and was not easily replaced.

THE AFTERMATH

THE JACOBITE RETREAT

Even as de Lauzun was conducting his staged withdrawal to the Naul, the first fragmented news of the defeat reached Dublin in the form of stragglers from the right-wing cavalry regiments who, having broken through and scattered the Jacobite foot as it gathered to cross the bridge at Duleek, had fled towards the capital, arriving in the city some time around 5.00pm.

For the next few hours, and as the number of fugitives grew, rumour and counter-rumour flew, alternately increasing and decreasing the magnitude of the Jacobite defeat. The rumour became fact upon the arrival of King James and his escort at Dublin Castle during the early evening.

In an apocryphal encounter, James is quoted as having met Lady Tyrconnel, who is then said to have asked the king if he were hungry, to which the response was 'after the breakfast which I have been served, I have even less stomach for supper', an obvious reference to the battle. Another writer has James saying to Lady Tyrconnel 'Madam, your countrymen run well' to which the rejoinder is said to have been 'Yes it would seem so, but Your Majesty would appear to have won the race'. The inference is plain as to where James felt the reason from his defeat lay. During a meeting of the Privy Council, James effectively conceded defeat, continuing in his tirade against his Irish troops:

> *When it came to a trial they basely fled the field and left the spoil to the enemy, nor could they be prevailed upon to rally, though the loss in the whole defeat was but inconsiderable; so that henceforward, I nevermore determine to head an Irish army. And do now resolve to shift for myself, and so gentlemen must you.*

The break was complete, and early in the morning of 2 July James rode southwards from Dublin towards Bray. There he inexplicably ordered his escort to remain behind to deter any pursuit and, with one or two companions, he continued to Duncannon Fort, near Waterford. There he boarded a French frigate which took him to Kinsale, and from there he took a ship for France and lifelong exile.

FROM DULEEK TO DUBLIN

With the enemy in full retreat, the Williamites were not inclined to push their initial pursuit of the enemy too vigorously for three main reasons: Firstly, most regiments had been in action for several hours and needed

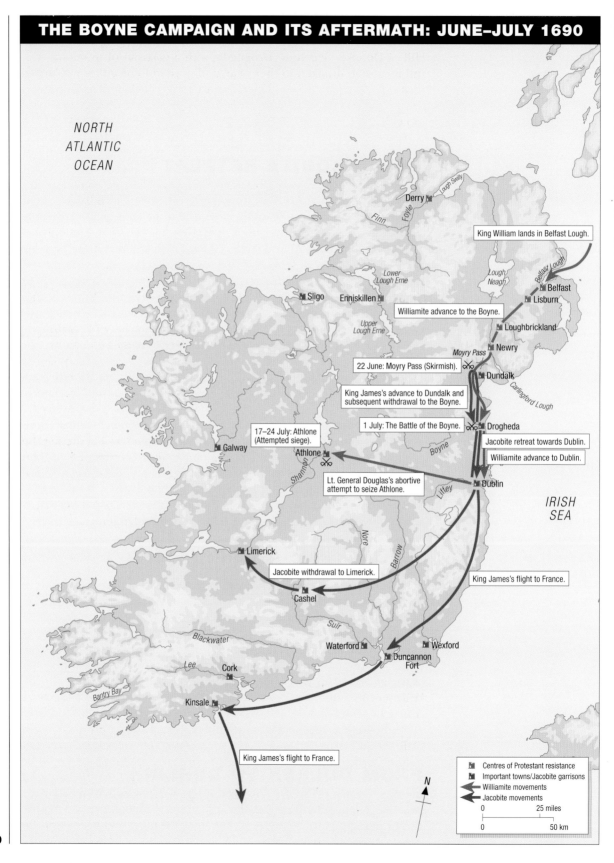

NORTH
ATLANTIC
OCEAN

King William lands in Belfast Lough.

Williamite advance to the Boyne.

22 June: Moyry Pass (Skirmish).

King James's advance to Dundalk and
subsequent withdrawal to the Boyne.

1 July: The Battle of the Boyne.

17–24 July: Athlone
(Attempted siege).

Lt. General Douglas's abortive
attempt to seize Athlone.

Jacobite retreat towards Dublin.

Williamite advance to Dublin.

King James's flight to France.

Jacobite withdrawal to Limerick.

King James's flight to France.

Derry

Lough Swilly

Foyle

Finn

Lower
Lough Erne

Upper
Lough Erne

Sligo

Enniskillen

Lough
Neagh

Belfast Lough

Belfast

Lisburn

Loughbrickland

Newry

Moyry Pass

Dundalk

Carlingford Lough

Drogheda

Galway

Athlone

Shannon

Boyne

Dublin

Liffey

IRISH
SEA

Limerick

Nore

Barrow

Cashel

Suir

Blackwater

Waterford

Wexford

Duncannon
Fort

Lee

Cork

Bantry Bay

Kinsale

N

Centres of Protestant resistance
Important towns/Jacobite garrisons
Williamite movements
Jacobite movements

0   25 miles
0   50 km

90

to rest, in addition to which, the reserve foot had only crossed the Boyne sometime between 2.00 and 3.00pm, and was still coming up across the Hill of Donore. Secondly, Drogheda, with a garrison of unknown size, still remained untaken to their rear, and needed to be either masked or secured. Thirdly, the bottleneck at Duleek, which had so hindered the Jacobite retreat, also prevented William's forces from advancing too quickly.

Once the lack of an enemy pursuit became apparent, the rout slowed and a few miles north of Dublin, Berwick was able to rally a number of men. In his diary, John Stevens, an officer with the Grand Prior's Regiment, wrote: 'there being now left together the colours of only five of six regiments and at first halting not above 100 men in all, although before morning we were much increased, sentinels being placed on the road to turn all soldiers into the field'.

At daybreak, this ad-hoc force continued to Dublin where Berwick pitched camp in the fields to the north of the city. Here, regimental officers planted their colours in an effort to rally the stragglers where they could be contained and assigned to their units without their having to invoke the curiosity of the local population.

Skirting the city, the column marched for the hamlet of Kilmainham, where most of the troops believed the army would re-form and in combination with local militias and the city garrison either defend the city or once again engage the Williamites in a pitched battle, but it was too late

As they approached Dublin, several of the senior French officers upon whom the command of the army had now devolved left their posts, apparently in an effort to find de Lauzun, who had ridden ahead in an attempt to establish a route by which the troops could avoid entering the capital. They did not find de Lauzun, and instead continued to Dublin where they met with King James and fled with him to the coast and thence to France.

With no overall direction, and despite the successful withdrawal from the Boyne, the Jacobite army simply disintegrated, with regiments scattered and much needed equipment lost. Turning west, these fugitives marched – via Cashel – for the Shannon and safety where they could re-form and fight another day. The Irish horse were quite rightly lauded for their efforts in delaying the Williamite crossings whilst their infantry counterparts were derided for what was incorrectly perceived as a total collapse. Likewise, several officers – Berwick, Sheldon, Hamilton, Boisseleau and Zurlauben among them – had their reputations enhanced, whereas others such as Léry de Girardin or La Hoguette would find that their actions would come under close scrutiny at Versailles. Alone stands de Lauzun, whose overreaction in the initial stages of the battle was the catalyst for the Williamite victory but without whose calmness under pressure, the retreat could have degenerated into disaster.

As William observed the final flight of the Jacobite horse at Platin Hall, he immediately took stock of the situation: although he could neither have predicted the Jacobite overreaction to the threat posed by the combined forces of Schomberg and Douglas, nor have anticipated the dogged persistence of Tyrconnell's troopers in disputing the river crossings his plan had succeeded.

His immediate problem, however, was how to stage a pursuit of the fleeing enemy, with the small number of troops to hand, most of whom had been in combat since crossing the river at Mill Ford, whilst at the same time consolidating his army's position.

Leaving sufficient troops to cover Drogheda, the army centre, now under Württemburg-Neustadt, advanced into positions between Duleek and Donore whilst William pressed forward at the head of the left-wing cavalry.

Arriving at Duleek, he found the town in Schomberg's possession, and a force was detached to follow up the James's army and to ensure that it did not reform. Precious time was lost as the troops had to negotiate the Magdalene Bridge that had so delayed the Irish regiments but eventually they set out. Contact was made with de Lauzun's rearguard after it had negotiated the ford across the Naul but it was obvious to William that, in the fading light, and without adequate support, no progress could be made against an enemy who had chosen another river line to defend. Having ensured that the enemy retreat continued, he pulled his troops back to Duleek where they camped for the evening.

On the following day, de la Melonière, with a mixed force of Anglo-Danes – as a precursor to siege operations – summoned the Jacobite garrison of Drogheda to surrender. Like many on both sides, he was therefore surprised when Lord Iveagh, instead of even mounting a token defence conceded defeat, being allowed to march his troops unarmed to Athlone whilst surrendering a considerable amount of much-needed supplies to William's soldiers.

With Drogheda secure, the march on Dublin could continue and on 3 July, as William approached the city from the north he was met by a deputation of prominent Protestant citizens who, with the departure of the Jacobite forces felt that it was safe to request that he place the city under his protection.

Two battalions of the *Gardes te Voet* were detailed to occupy the city and maintain order, whilst the rest of the army remained outside of the city precincts. For two days the troops rested and on Sunday, William formally entered the city in triumph – a Te Deum was sung at St Patrick's Cathderal, whilst all over the city, bonfires were lit in celebration.

The following day, Monday 7 July, William reviewed his army at Finglas, a few miles north of Dublin and here, convinced that the Jacobites had been utterly defeated, he made his single great error of the campaign. In what has become known as the 'Finglas Declaration', he set out his conditions for a settlement with the defeated enemy – instead of attempting to come to terms with the enemy leaders and playing upon their dissatisfaction with James, he decided to threaten them, stating that their lands and properties would be forfeit unless he was satisfied as to their 'penitence'.

William did not quantify how he would be satisfied as to the sincerity of any newly found loyalties on the part of former Jacobites, and thus rather than driving a wedge between the various factions within the enemy camp, he only served to unite them, in such a way as to persuade them to continue to fight until the bitter end; an end which would come at the walls of Limerick, over a year in the future.

THE BATTLEFIELD TODAY

In December 1999, the Irish government set up an initiative to repurchase the battlefield from individual landowners and develop the area to reflect its importance both in Irish and European history. The site is being developed by the Irish government's Office of Public Works in consultation with various local and cross-border organizations, such as the Grand Orange Lodge of Ireland, all of whom have a committed interest in the battlefield.

The site itself, based around the former Oldbridge Estate, is accessible and fully signposted from the following routes L21 (Donore), M1 (Dublin–Belfast), N1 (Drogheda) and N2 (Slane–Ashbourne). It is open to the public from May to September each year from 10.00am to 6.00pm, although larger groups can be catered for outside of this period by prior appointment.

The main area, around the Oldbridge Estate, is covered by some 4km of walkways which are covered by a series of illustrated information panels, written in English and Irish, placed in locations which were prominent during the course of the battle, such as the Jacobite and Williamite camps at Donore and Tullyallen, respectively. In order to allow visitors to follow the chronology of the battle, each of the information panels shows the approximate time at which the action took place. The walkways can be traversed on a 'self-guiding' basis or as part of an organized tour by the estate managers.

In addition, there are various weapons on display, including pikes, firearms and both scale-model and full-size artillery pieces.

On every Sunday during the months of June to September, there is also a programme of living history displays which include contemporary cavalry drill and the firing of 'black powder' weapons.

The site is in a state of continual progress and, as such, the Office of Public Works is in constant communication with local authorities to improve access for the public, as this is fundamental to the future development of the battlefield. More up-to-date information can be obtained from the official website www.battleoftheboyne.ie or via email on battleoftheboyne@opw.ie.

GOVERNMENT INFORMATION SERVICES,
DEPARTMENT OF THE TAOISEACH,
GOVERNMENT BUILDINGS, DUBLIN 2.
TEL: 01 662 4422 FAX: 01 678 9037
LO CALL 1890 422 622

SEIRBHÍSÍ EOLAIS AN RIALTAIS,
ROINN AN TAOISIGH,
TITHE AN RIALTAIS, BAILE ÁTHA CLIATH 2.
TEIL: 01 662 4422 FAX: 01 678 9037
GLAO ÁITIÚIL 1890 422 622

Taoiseach Announces Major Initiative on Battle of the Boyne Site

The Taoiseach, Mr. Bertie Ahern, T.D., announced today that the Government has agreed in principle to purchase the site of the Battle of the Boyne and to develop it in a way which fully reflects its huge historical importance and its significance for all of the people of the island, and in particular of course for the unionist tradition. The Taoiseach said:

"The Battle of the Boyne was one of the most important events in our island's history, and indeed had a wider European significance. It should be remembered and understood by all of us.

In this historic week when the institutions of the Good Friday Agreement have been established, we must dedicate ourselves to promoting mutual respect and reconciliation. In particular, the Agreement commits the Government to 'continue to take further active steps to demonstrate its respect for the different traditions on the island of Ireland'.

I am glad, therefore, to announce that the Government have agreed in principle to purchase the site of the Battle of the Boyne. A special inter-Departmental committee, established by my colleague the Minister for Foreign Affairs, David Andrews, T.D., has been tasked with bringing forward comprehensive long-term proposals for the development of the site. We are spending £150,000 on immediate interim measures to improve public access, visitor facilities and information material."

The Taoiseach added: "In opening up this hugely important part of our shared heritage to the people of the island and to overseas visitors, the Government will continue to consult closely with representatives of the unionist tradition, with the relevant local authorities and with community groups."

BIBLIOGRAPHY

For those who would read further on the Boyne campaign and the Williamite War of 1689–91, I would recommend both Jacobite Ireland by J. G. Simms and 1690 The Battle of the Boyne by Padraig Lenihan. A full list of the works consulted during the research of this book follows:

Adamson, Ian, *1690 – William & the Boyne* (Belfast, 1995)

Aubrey, Philip, *The Defeat of James Stuart's Armada, 1692* (Leicester, 1979)

Bartlett, Thomas and Jeffery, Keith (eds), *A Military History of Ireland* (Cambridge, 1996)

Belloc, Hilaire, *James the Second* (Philadelphia, 1928)

Berresford Ellis, Peter, *The Boyne Water – The Battle of the Boyne 1690* (Belfast, 1976)

Boulger, Demetrius Charles, *The Battle of the Boyne* (London, 1911)

Bredin, Brigadier A.E.C., *A History of the Irish Soldier* (Belfast, 1987)

Brereton, J.M., *A History of the 4th/7th Dragoon Guards* (Catterick, 1982)

Caufield, Richard (ed), *Journal of the Very Rev. Rowland Davies, LL.D, Dean of Ross &c* (London, 1857)

Childs, John, *The Army, James II and the Glorious Revolution* (Manchester, 1980)

—, *The British Army of William III, 1689–1702* (Manchester, 1987)

Clarke, James S., *The Life of James the Second, King of England &c* (London, 1816)

Clifford, Brendan (ed), *Derry and the Boyne* (Belfast, 1990)

D'Alton, John, *King James's Irish Army List (1689)* (Limerick, 1997)

Danaher, K. and Simms, J.G. (eds), *The Danish Force in Ireland, 1690–1691* (Dublin, 1962)

Doherty, Richard, *The Williamite War in Ireland 1688–1691* (Dublin, 1998)

Ede-Borrett, Stephen, *The Army of James II, Uniforms & Organisation* (Leeds, 1987)

Gibson, Oliver C., *The Western Protestant Army – Ireland 1688/90* (Omagh, 1989)

Gilbert, John T. (ed), *A Jacobite Narrative of the War in Ireland 1688–1691* (Shannon, 1971)

Grew, Marion, *William Bentinck and William III* (London, 1924)

Haddick-Flynn, Kevin, *Sarsfield & the Jacobites* (Dublin, 2003)

Hays-McCoy, Gerald A., *Irish Battles* (London, 1969)

Hayton, D.W. and O'Brien, G. (eds), *War and Politics in Ireland, 1649–1730* (London, 1986)

Hennessy, Maurice, *The Wild Geese* (London, 1973)

Hewitson, Anthony, *Diary of Thomas Bellingham – An Officer under William III* (Preston, 1908)

Holmes, Richard, *War Walks 2* (London, 1997)

Irish Manuscripts Commission, *Négotiations de M. Le Comte d'Avaux en Irlande 1689–90*, 2 vols (Dublin, 1934 and 1958)

Israel, Jonathan, *The Dutch Republic – Its Rise, Greatness and Fall 1477–1806* (Oxford, 1995)

Kemmy, Jim and Walsh, Larry (eds), *The Old Limerick Journal: 1690 Siege Edition* (Limerick, 1990)

Kinross, John, *The Boyne & Aughrim – The War of the Two Kings* (Moreton-in-Marsh, 1998)

Lenihan, Pádraig, *1690 – Battle of the Boyne* (Stroud, 2003)

Lossky, Andrew, *Louis XIV & the French Monarchy* (New Brunswick, 1994)

Lynn, John A., *Giant of the Grand Siècle: The French Army 1610–1715* (Cambridge, 1997)

—, *The Wars of Louis XIV* (London, 1999)

Macaulay, Thomas Babington, Lord, *A History of England from the Accession of James II* (New York, 1880)

MacCartney-Filgate, Edward, 'A Staff Ride in the Valley of the Boyne', *Cornhill Magazine* (London, 1907)

McConnell, Charles, *The Siege of Carrickfergus* (Carrickfergus, 2000)

Macrory, Patrick, *The Siege of Derry* (London, 1980)

Maguire, W.A. (ed), *Kings in Conflict – The Revolutionary War in Ireland and its Aftermath 1689–1750* (Belfast, 1990)

Mulloy, Sheila (ed), *Franco-Irish Correspondence, Dec. 1688–Feb. 1692*, 3 vols. (Dublin, 1983)

Murray, R.H. (ed), *The Journal of John Stevens* (Oxford, 1912)

Nosworthy, Brent, *The Anatomy of Victory: Battle Tactics 1689–1763* (New York, 1992)

O'Callaghan, John Cornelius, *Irish Brigades in the Service of France* (Shannon, 1968)

O'Carroll, Colonel Donal, 'An indifferent good post: the battlefield of the Boyne', *Irish Sword*, Vol XVIII, No. 70 (Dublin, 1990)

Ò Ciardha, Éamonn, *Ireland and the Jacobite Cause, 1685–1766: A Fatal Attachment* (Dublin, 2002)

O'Kelly, Charles, *The Jacobite War in Ireland (1688–1691)* (Dublin, 1896)

Parker, Robert, *Memoirs of the most remarkable military transactions from the year 1683 &c* (London, 1747)

Petrie, Sir Charles, *The Marshal Duke of Berwick* (London, 1953)

—, *The Great Tyrconnel* (Dublin, 1972)

Read, Charles A. and Waddington, Francis (eds), *Mémoires inédits de Dumont de Bostaquet, Gentilhomme Normand &c* (Paris, 1864)

Riegler Frederick J., *Anglo-Catholics, the Army of Ireland and the Jacobite War*, 2 vols (PhD thesis, Temple University, USA, 1983)

Rousset, Camille, *Histoire de Louvois et son administration politique et militaire* (Paris, 1891)

Sapherson, Alan, *The Dutch Army of William III* (Leeds, 1997)

—, *The British Army of William III* (Leeds, 1997)

—, *William III at War – Scotland and Ireland 1689–1691* (Leeds, 2001)

Sells, A. Lytton, *The Memoirs of James II – His Campaigns as Duke of York 1652–1660* (London, 1962)

Sergeant, Philip W., *Little Jennings and Fighting Dick Talbot*, 2 vols (London, 1913)

Shepherd, Robert, *Ireland's Fate – The Boyne and After* (London, 1990)

Simms, J.G., *Jacobite Ireland* (Dublin, 2000)

Stapleton, John M. Jr, *Importing the Military Revolution: William III, the Glorious Revolution, and the Rise of the Standing Army in Britain, 1688–1712* (MA thesis, Ohio State University, 1994)

Story, George, *A true and impartial history of the affairs of Ireland &c* (London, 1691)

Todhunter, John, *The Life of Patrick Sarsfield* (Dublin, 1895)

Walker, H.M., *A History of the Northumberland Fusiliers 1674–1902* (London, 1919)

Wauchope, Piers, *Patrick Sarsfield and the Williamite War* (Dublin, 1992)

Webb, Lieutenant Colonel E.A.H., *History of the 12th (The Suffolk Regiment 1685–1913)* (London, 1914)

—, *History of the 17th (The Leicestershire Regiment)* (London, 1911)

INDEX